P9-DDO-487

A TECHNOLOGY OF READING AND WRITING

Volume 1

**Learning to Read and Write:
A Task Analysis**

EDUCATIONAL PSYCHOLOGY

Allen J. Edwards, Series Editor
Department of Psychology
Southwest Missouri State University
Springfield, Missouri

Phillip S. Strain, Thomas P. Cooke, and Tony Apolloni. Teaching Exceptional Children: Assessing and Modifying Social Behavior
Donald E. P. Smith and others. A Technology of Reading and Writing (in four volumes).

> Vol. 1. *Learning to Read and Write: A Task Analysis (by Donald E. P. Smith)*
> Vol. 2. *Criterion-Referenced Tests for Reading and Writing (by Judith M. Smith, Donald E. P. Smith, and James R. Brink)*
> Vol. 3. *The Adaptive Classroom (by Donald E. P. Smith)*
> Vol. 4. *Preparing Instructional Tasks (by Donald E. P. Smith)*

In preparation:

Gilbert R. Austin. Early Childhood Education: An International Perspective
Joel R. Levin and Vernon L. Allen (eds.). Cognitive Learning in Children: Theories and Strategies
Vernon L. Allen (ed.). Children as Teachers: Theory and Research on Tutoring
António Simões (ed.). The Bilingual Child: Research and Analysis of Existing Educational Themes
Erness Bright Brody and Nathan Brody. Intelligence: Nature, Determinants, and Consequences

A TECHNOLOGY OF READING AND WRITING

Volume 1

Learning to Read and Write: A Task Analysis

Donald E. P. Smith

School of Education
The University of Michigan
Ann Arbor, Michigan

ACADEMIC PRESS   New York   San Francisco   London   1976

A Subsidiary of Harcourt Brace Jovanovich, Publishers

ACADEMIC PRESS, INC.
111 Fifth Avenue, New York, New York 10003

United Kingdom Edition published by
ACADEMIC PRESS, INC. (LONDON) LTD.
24/28 Oval Road, London NW1

Library of Congress Cataloging in Publication Data

Smith, Donald E.   P
        Learning to read and write.

        (A technology of reading and writing ; v. 1) (Educa-
tional psychology series)
        Bibliography: p.
        Includes index.
        1.   Reading.   2.   Children—Writing.   3.   Discrimina-
tion learning.   4.   Paired-association learning.   I.   Title.
LB1050.S572   vol. 1   372.6s   [372.6]   75-30473
ISBN 0–12–651701–0

CONTENTS

Preface   ix

Introduction   1

    I. Purpose   1
   II. The Subject Matter   2
  III. The Title   3
  IV. The Content   4
   V. The Structure   5

1

Learning to Read and Write   7

    I. The Process of Reading and Writing   7
   II. Why the Process Fails   15
  III. Some Definitions   21

2

Learning as a Discrimination Process   25

    I. Discrimination Learning   27
   II. The Learning Target   27
  III. Kinds of Learned Responses   31
  IV. Relationships among Discriminative Responses   35
   V. Conditions Required for Learning Discriminative Responses   37

3

Modality, Level, and Sequence   41

    I. Single-Modality and Cross-Modality Processes   44
   II. Responses in a Cross-Modality System   46
  III. Objectives in a Cross-Modality System   47
  IV. Task Characteristics   48
   V. Level and Sequence   53
  VI. Implications of the Model   56

4

Processing Stimuli   59

    I. Establishing the Learning Target   60
   II. Cross-Modality or Substitution Learning   64
  III. Central Processing and Eye Movements   67

5

**Processing Information during
Reading and Writing**   77

    I. The Time Frame: The Specious Present   78
   II. Mechanisms of Information Processing   79
  III. Implications of a Three-Level, Cross-Modality Model   85

6

Measuring Competence in Reading and Writing   99

    I. The Domain of Reading   100
   II. Criterion-Referenced Tests   103
  III. The Impact of Measurement on Achievement   110

7

Motivation as Attentional Control — 113

   I. Learner Conditions — 115
  II. Environmental Conditions — 116
 III. Behavior Modification as Self-Shaping — 118

8

Information Feedback in Educational Systems — 121

   I. Feedback Defined — 122
  II. System Defined — 123
 III. Engineering a School Innovation — 125

APPENDIX A

Task Synthesis — 139

   I. Type I: Recognition — 139
  II. Type II: Reproduction — 143
 III. Type III: Substitution — 145

APPENDIX B

Expanded Interlocking Model — 151

References — 155

Index — 159

PREFACE

The process by which children learn to read and write has proved a fascinating puzzle to investigators. Indeed, it has absorbed the scientific lifetimes of scores of psychologists and has been accorded more than passing interest by linguists, neurologists, and sociologists. One must be impressed by the sheer volume of experimental work that has appeared since 1920. In their recent book, Eleanor Gibson and Harry Levin have organized and reviewed more than 700 articles and books, most of them published in the past 10 years (*The Psychology of Reading,* M.I.T. Press, 1975).

Certainly efforts to explicate the process are justified. All school learning may be viewed as learning to read, write, listen to, and speak the language—of science, of mathematics, of social studies, even of art, music, and physical education. For language is the great controller of human behavior.

Fortunately, today's investigators have available to them tools that were only dimly perceived in the 1920s:

- a technology of behavior, provided by B. F. Skinner
- a behavioral analysis of language, provided by Kenneth Pike
- a behavioral psychology of perception, provided by James J. Gibson

The genius of each of these men has led him to focus on **observable behavior** and to construct his science **outside the skin** of the behaving organism. One result is that the technician need not become lost in the maze of clever constructs characterizing psychology and linguistics. More important, the phenomena reported by each are sufficiently analogous to provide a basis for a science of language.

By sheerest accident, it fell my lot to interact with each of these men at critical periods of my work:

As a doctoral student at Cornell University in 1950–1951, I took courses with J. J. Gibson. One day, as I was passing his office, he called me in (to serve as a naive observer). He was holding three small pieces of cardboard, each containing apparently random marks made by a stylus. He said, "Tell me what you see here." Since projective tests were the rage in those days, I said, "That one looks like a man on a trapeze . . ." "NO!" he shouted. "Those look like random marks—and that's because they **are** random marks!" And that was my introduction to psychology as a science.

In 1957, I spent time with B. F. Skinner at Harvard University, at the request of a publishing house interested in "teaching machines." The analysis of behavior that he demonstrated was brilliant. Even more impressive to me, a former teacher, was the **stimulus control of behavior** which he had achieved and which should be possible with children.

In 1966, I sat in the coffee room of the psychology department at the University of Michigan in casual conversation with a stranger. He described his analysis of an Indian language using the rotational method of factor analysis. But he was rotating **phonemes** as factors and by that means revealed the grammatical structure of the language. No, he had not heard of factor analysis: His field was linguistics. It was the most ingenious demonstration of problem solving I had ever witnessed. This was Kenneth Pike, the author of "tagmemics," a behavioral analysis of language.

The contributions of these men to a science of language behavior have been enormous. Without them, our present effort would be much less than it is.

* * * * *

Co-author of the ideas in this volume is Judith Meyer Smith, who is principal author also of Volumes 2 and 4. Even more, she is my colleague, friend, wife, mother of four very literate children, and prolific producer of effective learning materials.

This book is the first of four volumes. It describes the learning-to-read process from a behavioral engineering point of view. Volume 2, *Criterion-Referenced Tests for Reading and Writing,* specifies literate behavior as test items articulated with the theory of Volume 1. Volume 3, *The Adaptive Classroom,* provides procedures by which common methods of teaching reading and writing can be engineered to produce mastery behavior. Finally, Volume 4, *Preparing Instructional Tasks,* trains teachers to build tasks which teach the test items of Volume 2.

A minimum standard of literacy for this book was reached by trying out successive versions with my students in reading theory and instructional systems. I am deeply indebted to them for requiring me to explain myself. The last draft was read for substance by former colleagues, Carl Semmelroth, Dale Brethower, and Tim Walters, each of whom, as judged by their editing, know my position better than I do.

Finally, I have been delighted by the editorial and packaging skills of the staff at Academic Press.

INTRODUCTION

A family I know exhibits a curious characteristic: On the way to the car each morning, the father carries a briefcase. He is followed by his wife, who carries a briefcase; she is followed by a teenaged daughter—who carries a briefcase. Three more children follow, and the youngest carries a satchel—which looks like a briefcase. Having discriminated something, we tend to reproduce it.

I have spent most of the last 15 years constructing learning tasks, observing children responding to tasks, thinking about stimulus arrays, responses, feedback, and the like, mostly within the context of teaching the process of learning to read and write. I have talked to colleagues and read their writings; in so doing I have made a number of discriminations.

I. Purpose

This book is an attempt to reproduce those discriminations. It is a kind of handbook of behavioral engineering, a description of how one might view the world of children and language and instructional tasks in order to promote language achievement. It would probably be most interesting to people who prepare instructional environments, especially those who work with learning tasks in reading, writing, listening, and speaking. These people would include behavioral psychologists, authors of instructional materials, and teachers.

The scope of this book is limited in two directions: It is only partly theoretical and only partly applied. Throughout, I have tried to provide enough illustrations so that readers can recognize and produce effective tasks, and enough theoretical rationale so that they can see why such tasks should work. (For further delineation of skills, tasks and methods, see Volumes 2, 3, and 4 of this series.)

II. The Subject Matter

I am concerned here with how learning to read and write can be engineered. **Learning to read** is not the same as the **reading process** of mature literates. Differences between learning to read and reading are analogous to the differences between the behaviors of learners and experts in other skills, such as walking, riding a bicycle, analyzing discourse—even explicating the learning-to-read process.

First steps are hard won and are marked by frustration, error, resistance to continuing, regressions, shortcuts that do not work, insights, excitement. Later increments in skill occur almost automatically, simply because the learner has attacked more and more complex problems.

I clearly remember an incident that to me constituted learning to read. My first-grade teacher had said, "Try to read the first story." The first word was *the* and I knew it. But the second word was new: *bird*. After two or three abortive attempts at sounding it, I noticed a picture at the top of the page—a tree with apples and a bird. BIRD! That was what those noises had sounded like! "Oh-ho!" I said to myself, "You're supposed to make sounds and guess!" On the preceding day I could not read the comic page. That day, I read "all by myself." Learning to read came in a rush, or so my memories would have it.

On the other hand, learning **how** reading can be learned has come painfully slowly, over a period of 25 years. The first 10 years were spent searching for the right tools. It took 10 more years to learn how to use those tools, that is, how to construct a "learning-to-read machine," a programmed curriculum that would produce literate behavior dependably. The last 5 years have been spent trying to describe the process to others.

The right tools of any science include observation skills and a knowledge of theory construction. Appropriate use of these tools yields data, concepts, and principles. But just as a knowledge of the concepts and principles of physics is insufficient preparation for building a bridge, a knowledge of the behavior of children, however derived, is insufficient preparation for inducing learning behavior. The missing tool is a **technology**. In this case, the tool is a technology of learning: systematic techniques derived from and consistent with scientific principles but designed to solve concrete problems.

This instructional technology has developed rapidly in the past 20 years, largely because of the contributions of B. F. Skinner (1957a) and his students. The methods of task analysis and task synthesis now available make possible a relatively complete, though primitive, description of how the illiterate child can achieve literate status.

This book, then, is a description of learning to read and write from an engineering point of view. To return to my bridge-building analogy, that could mean that I will describe how to build a bridge. But that is not what I propose to do. Rather, having built a bridge (having engineered one kind of learning-to-read process), I shall now try to describe the concepts, definitions, ways of viewing behavior, and ways of viewing the language that make it possible to engineer literate behavior. I am concerned, then, with facilitating the efforts of others who will build better bridges.

III.   The Title

The title of this book includes the subtitle *A Task Analysis.* Faced with a problem of skill deficiency, the developer of training materials carries out a task analysis. He first determines the **response capabilities** of the learner. (Response capabilities include both previously mastered skills and other responses humans are capable of making under adequate conditions.) Then he searches within the content of the skill to be learned for structural units to which responses can be made by the learner (in behavioral terms, "the kinds of stimuli in the presence of which those responses are emitted"). The synthesis might then consist of matching responses to structures, of matching appropriate behaviors to the units of content to be mastered.

In the case of a language student, analysis of response capabilities yields the response forms of listening, speaking, reading, and writing. **Initial** stimuli are spoken sentences and words.

Analysis of task content yields component parts of the content—the specific stimuli to be used—and some unique arrangement of them. For example, analysis of a language yields a series of structural units: letter groups, words, phrases, sentences, and paragraphs. The words consist of particular letter groups arranged in a particular order; phrases consist of particular words in a particular order, and so on.

Relationships between content and response may be expressed as a matching of a behavior to a unit of content, a function to a structure. For example, one matches the function or response *saying* to the structural unit, *a word;* the response *draw* is matched to the structural unit, *a letter.* But there is more to a task analysis than this simplified description. What constitutes the "more" justifies the writing of the book.

IV. The Content

In drafting the chapters of this book, I was struck with the regularity with which the content of a new chapter brought to mind a particular child who led the way. It is as though the trail to literate behavior were blazed by Belinda and Bob and Zack and Dan. Since these children provided the problems that led to new ways of viewing the process, of learning to read and write, it seems both ethically correct and pedagogically sound to begin those chapters with their stories.

THE CONCEPT

What also became increasingly clear in the writing was the evolution of a concept of what is learned. Although it seemed common sense to view all learning tasks as containing stimuli to be discriminated and responses to be differentiated, there gradually emerged an entity I began to call the **learning target**, the actual product of learning.

The only reality is in the learner. He constructs his percepts from the data of experience and he responds in ways that will reproduce those percepts in his external environment. Thus, the learning target is what is learned, the percept. How it is learned is essentially a discriminative process. **Independent learning** consists of identifying missing percepts—those not yet in one's repertoire—and developing them by means of self-shaping, the applying of reinforcers and punishers to oneself on the basis of similarity of match between the developing percept and what is perceived from the environment.

A derived concept concerns the structure of language. Language learning tasks must be both representative of the language and doable by learners. Tasks are constrained, therefore, both by the regularities of the language and by the capabilities of the learner. We must view the structure of language as a reflection of the processing functions of learners. **The learner cannot deal with phenomena he cannot perceive.** Many logically correct descriptions of language simply do not fit the perceptual or cognitive processes used in learning. The resolution of this problem is a taxonomy of language I shall call the **language domain**. As it stands, it conforms reasonably well both to the concepts of linguistics, as described by linguistic scientists, and to language tasks, as described by reading specialists, but with some distinctive differences.

THE ENGINEERING STRATEGIES

The models of learning processes presented are designed to facilitate the construction of learning systems. The book is replete with paradigms for constructing tasks. As I have said, it is something of an engineering handbook, reflecting not "the state of the art" (Galanter, 1959) but rather the state of the technology as practiced by people who do discrimination programming.

ASSUMPTIONS

When my colleagues and I began to construct a learning-to-read program, we laid out a series of position statements that may be viewed either as assumptions in and of themselves or as implying assumptions about children:

(1) Any child who speaks English can learn to read what he says.
(2) Any learning task failed by the child may be viewed as an inappropriate task rather than as a deficiency of the child.
(3) Any learning task passed by fewer than 95% of the target population can be analyzed into its components and can be reconstructed to reach the 95% criterion.
(4) No child shall begin a new series of tasks until he has achieved a 100% score on the prior criterion test.

These dicta were adhered to rigidly. The 100% score on criterion tests should probably be adjusted to 80–85% in normal situations. For development purposes, it forced us early on to analyze system factors, especially teacher and classroom variables that might interfere with progress. When a child failed to progress despite what appeared to be adequate tasks, we looked to the learning system for answers.

V. The Structure

Chapter 1 describes how children learn to name and draw pictures and to read and write words. It then describes failures of the process attributable to skill deficiencies, performance deficiencies, and system factors.

Chapter 2 describes discrimination learning. It defines the learning target and describes three kinds of learning: **recognition, reproduction,** and **substitution**. It also gives task conditions for facilitating learning.

Chapter 3 introduces the concept of feedback within information-processing systems, both single-modality systems (such as vision) and cross-modality systems (visual input, auditory output). It includes task paradigms for multiple-step learning and introduces the concept of an alternating, interlocking pattern of skill development.

Chapter 4 describes stimulus processing; uncertainty reduction; a discriminative paradigm for cross-modality, paired-associate learning; and visual processing during reading.

Chapter 5 presents a hierarchical, cross-modality, information-processing model with operating rules based on uncertainty arousal and uncertainty reduction. Implications of the model are drawn and illustrated with a variety of problems and problem resolutions.

Chapter 6 presents the domain of reading skills arranged to show their relationships to one another and the order in which they are mastered by learners. Criterion-referenced tests for some of the 24 skill entries of the hierarchy are named. (The tests will be found in Volume 2.)

Chapter 7 draws together learner characteristics and environmental conditions that account for much of what is meant by motivation.

And Chapter 8 defines learners and classrooms as **adaptive systems,** responsive to feedback signals. It demonstrates how adaptive systems can be engineered and describes system response to innovation as a discriminative learning process.

LEARNING TO READ AND WRITE

Learning to read looks like a complicated process—partly because so many responses are required.[1] On the other hand, for the 6-year-old, reading and writing single words (if that is reading) is not much more complex than the process of naming and drawing pictures is for the 2- to 4-year-old. Learning to read and write words has much in common with learning to name and draw pictures.

I. The Process of Reading and Writing

A. *Naming and Drawing Pictures*

When the 2-year-old interacts with pictures, he takes several steps:

(*1*) He looks at the picture, hears its name, and says the name.
(*2*) He confuses the picture with other similar-appearing pictures and the name with other similar-sounding names. He has a discrimination deficit.

---

[1] My colleagues and I once counted the number of necessary tasks (or responses) in a complete program that began with letter and word discrimination and ended with sentence reading. We arrived at a total of 18,000 steps.

(*3*) When he corrects his errors, lines of the picture and sounds of the words become better defined, and he names the picture correctly more often.

(*4*) He tries to draw the picture, first by tracing or copying it, and later by drawing it from memory.

These four steps, (*1*) attending, (*2*) confusing and discriminating, (*3*) recognizing, and (*4*) reproducing are illustrated next, as a 2-year-old might follow them in the process of naming and drawing pictures.

ATTENDING

1

The child looks at a picture,
hears its name, and says the name.

He looks at a picture,   hears its name,   and says the name.

But, like you and me, 2-year-olds have problems.

Problem

To resolve these problems, he must discover some differences:

(*1*) how the pictured object differs from similar-appearing objects;
(*2*) how the object's name differs from similar-sounding names.

DISCRIMINATING

2

Objects differ from similar objects. Names differ from similar names.

RECOGNIZING

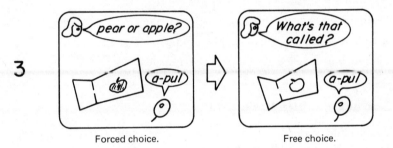

3

Forced choice.   Free choice.

By now, he can name the picture—first, with prompting (given two choices only: **forced choice**); then, without prompting (given unlimited possibilities: **free choice**).

REPRODUCING

4

Drawing by tracing,   by copying,   and from memory.

Finally, he may try drawing the picture, first by tracing or copying, later by drawing from memory.

The four steps taken to learn pictures and names are basically the same steps taken to learn reading and writing, and just about everything else that involves language:

Step 1   Looking at a picture, hearing its name, and repeating the name—we have called **attending** (or **attention**).

Step 2   Discovering ways pictures and the sounds of names differ from similar pictures and names—we have called **discriminating** (or **discrimination**).

Step 3   Naming the picture in a free choice situation—we have called **recognizing** (or **recognition**).

Step 4   Drawing a picture, from memory—we have called **reproducing** (or **reproduction**).

These steps are called by many different names:

Attending—listening to, looking at, observing, noticing, viewing, echoing, miming, surveying, imitating.

Discriminating—identifying, searching, matching, matching to sample.

Recognizing—knowing, naming, identifying, understanding, "reading."

Reproducing—drawing, writing, speaking, spelling,

B.   *Reading and Writing Words*

When a child learns to read and to write a word, he carries out the same steps—and in this order.[2]

1. HE ATTENDS TO THE WORD

Auditory   **Visual**

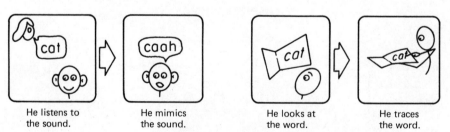

He listens to   He mimics   He looks at   He traces
the sound.   the sound.   the word.   the word.

---

[2] Steps that usually occur adventitiously are presented systematically here.

2. HE DISCRIMINATES THE WORD
Auditory

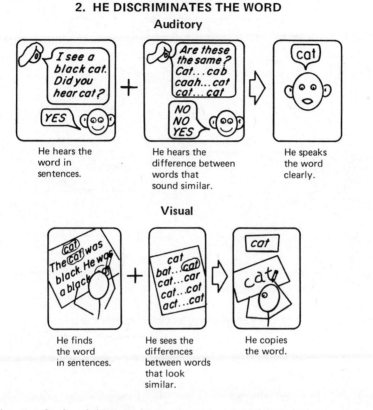

He hears the word in sentences.

He hears the difference between words that sound similar.

He speaks the word clearly.

Visual

He finds the word in sentences.

He sees the differences between words that look similar.

He copies the word.

To take step 3, the child must have taken steps 1 and 2 with these words: *cat, dog, I am a cat, I am a dog, I, am, a.* In step 3, hearing is viewed as auditory input, saying as auditory output.

3. HE RECOGNIZES THE WORD

Auditory in, Visual out

Visual in, Auditory out

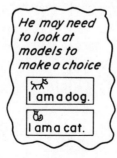

He sees and recognizes the word (as a picture) when he hears its name (forced choice).

He hears and recognizes the name of the word when he sees its picture (forced choice).

Visual and Auditory Matching

Reading

Free choice: silent reading test   Free choice: oral reading test

The reading shown here is the simplest form, the recognition of **sight words,** that is, words that do not require sounding out.

4. HE REPRODUCES THE WORD

He says the names
of the letters in
the word and draws   He reads the word
them.   to check his spelling.

Notice that in order to write (or spell) a word, it is helpful for the child to say letter names. He must be able to read and write (or draw) letters. But simply to read the word, he does not need to know his letters.

C. Decoding

Some may argue that knowing sight words is word calling rather than reading, and that the child may not really understand what he is reading. But recognizing sight words and responding to sentences consisting of sight words is actually a major step in learning to read. Most children need to master between 50 and 100 sight words in order to take the next major step, reading sentences containing unfamiliar words, words needing **decoding**.

Sight words are needed for at least three reasons:

(*1*) Such words as *of, the, was, which, after,* and *then*—a group of about 200 words that **connect** nouns and verbs and phrases and clauses—make up about 70% of the text of primary readers. These **function words** must be recognized quickly during reading in order to provide a context for the 3000 or more unknown words (Dolch, 1945).

(*2*) Many function words resist sounding out because they are phonemically irregular—they do not follow the rules of phonics. They are more easily learned as sight words.

(*3*) **Phonic chunks**, consonant–vowel combinations that have about the same sound in many different words, are used in sounding out words. The *ca* and the *at* in *cat* are chunks. These chunks or sound–symbol regularities are most easily used as tools when they are located **within** known words. So sight words can be used to teach the chunks of phonics. (Teachers call these chunks **phonograms** or **spelling patterns**.)

D. Decoding: Sounding Out and Context Guessing

Children learn many sight words by themselves, but sight words are not enough. Their acquisition by the learner is too slow to handle the 200,000 or more words in our language. The child is capable of using problem-solving strategies to unlock or decode printed words he does not recognize.

1. HE USES THE CONTEXT TO GENERATE POSSIBILITIES

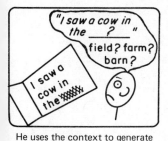

He uses the context to generate possible words.

He identifies a phonogram (chunk) and tries to match its sound with the sounds within the possibles.

He distorts the sound of the phonogram and finally achieves a match.

The context provides syntactic clues (*I saw a cow in the___* requires a noun) and semantic clues (*a cow in the___* requires the name of a place where one would expect to find a cow). Using the clues, the child generates possible words. Next, he identifies a part of the unrecognized word, usually the initial phonogram. He tries matching the sound of the initial phonogram with the initial sounds of his generated words. A match allows him to continue reading.

Sometimes the context provides so little information for generating possibilities that the child will use the initial phonogram for generating.

2. HE USES A PHONOGRAM TO GENERATE POSSIBILITIES

He meets an unre-cognized word and finds no context clues.

He identifies the first phonogram (*hor*) and generates words.

He identifies the last apparent phonogram (*ed*), and the sentence makes no sense.

He identifies the last phonogram (*fied*) and produces a distortion, recognizable as an appropriate word.

Decoding the unrecognized word proves too much for many children. To carry out this step, the child must be able to do the following:

(*1*) Use an average speaking vocabulary and recognize synonyms.

(*2*) Discriminate letters and letter names.

(*3*) Generate words as follows:

    (*a*) Given a syntactic signal requiring a noun or a verb or an adjective or an adverb, produce several words of the specified kind. For example, *He drove the car* (adverb).

    (*b*) Given a semantic signal requiring particular classes of words, produce several words that make sense.

    (*c*) Given a visual symbol (letter, letter group), produce a corresponding sound. Given a sound within a word, produce several words containing that sound in the same position (initial, medial, final).

    (*d*) Given a word, search it for the following parts: (*i*) known whole words (e.g., *play*ground); (*ii*) known beginnings or endings (e.g., *un*forgive*able*); (*iii*) known phonograms (e.g., h*ar*vest).

(*4*) Recognize common words on hearing distorted versions of them, such as occur when sounding out. For example, *horfied*.

(5) Use all these skills alone or in combination, as required, when faced with an unknown word.

This is a formidable list of skills. Most phonics systems used in schools devote most of their attention to item *3, c,* and somewhat less to item *3, d.* However, to be successful in reading, the child needs **all** these skills.

II. Why the Process Fails

The process of learning to read and write looks reasonably straightforward. Why should so many children fail? Only 70% become independent readers. Perhaps a look at the kinds of deficits children demonstrate will help identify reasons for failure.

A. *Basic Skill Deficiencies*

The term **basic skills** refers to a set of school-related auditory and visual responses often assumed to be in the repertoire of the child entering the first grade. In fact, they are not basic at all. If demonstrated by a 3-year-old, they would be called **advanced skills**. If one of these responses is missing, the child's learning efficiency will be impaired. If several are missing, the child may well end up on the discard pile. The commonly deficient skills may be grouped as **receptive** and **productive**, in the auditory and visual modalities.

AUDITORY RECEPTIVE SKILLS

The role played by auditory discrimination in the learning-to-read process is a subject of debate in the professional literature (see Samuels, 1971, for a review of the issue). Many linguists and some psychologists see little or no need for auditory discrimination training; other investigators have concluded that correlation coefficients of about .30 between measures of such skill and reading scores point to the probable usefulness of training.

The issue is not likely to be resolved either by rhetoric or by further laboratory studies. However, one way of resolving it is to apply an engineering paradigm:

(1) Identify a related task known to be a necessary step toward the final behavior. In this case, the related task might be matching rhyming words or counting the number of syllables in polysyllabic words.

(2) Identify children who are unable to accomplish that task and who are failing in reading.

(3) Provide whatever instruction is necessary to enable all the children to accomplish the task.

First attempts to help a failing group result in the construction of tasks that allow one or a few to move on to and succeed at the criterion task (such as matching rhyming words). Those children who do not succeed at the first tasks are given more basic instruction. A few of these children will then be able to move up to the criterion task. When the total group has passed the hurdle, what has been produced is a series of tasks that can be graded from lowest to highest. We can infer from these tasks a series of subskills that must be developed.

When one has carried out such a program with children who had been floundering, and these children begin to make progress—whereas other children not given the training or given placebos do not—one becomes increasingly confident of the role of the skills involved. The debate over whether auditory discrimination contributes to reading ability becomes academic. The laboratory evidence is not clear-cut for several reasons: inadequacies in measurement, difficulty in testing young children, time of year of testing, and the kind of correlation coefficient to be expected.

Auditory discrimination skills are critical early in the first grade. By the end of the first grade, as shown by Cabot (1968), most of the primitive children have made substantial gains. If the relationship between auditory discrimination skills and reading is investigated at that time, the size of the correlation coefficient (r) will be reduced, owing to a truncated distribution.[3] In the meantime, however, much damage may have been incurred by the children because of inattention and inadequate basic learnings.

One should expect a coefficient from .3 to .4 for the relationship between a global skill such as reading and its component skills. Children who lack a component skill will fail in reading, thus implying a correlation of +1.00. But children who have a component skill may or may not succeed, depending upon whether they have other component skills. For those children, the correlation could be as low as 0.00. Gradations of skill may result in a coefficient of another magnitude. When the relationships for children of varying skill are summed up, the .3 value seems reasonable and is reminiscent of similar findings in the vocational interest—academic ability relationship studied from 1930 to 1950 (Fryer, 1931).

The foregoing discussion has been necessary to emphasize that there is conflicting evidence on certain issues, and that we have evaluated the literature to unearth hypotheses **but not to resolve issues.** In all cases, the child has led us, i.e., empirical evidence from classroom try-outs of materials has been used in decision making. Now, we will return to the question of basic skill deficiencies, auditory.

---

[3] The symbol r indicates **relationship,** specifically a **Spearman** or **product—moment** coefficient of correlation. The value of r varies from high negative (−1.00) through no relationship (.00) to high positive (+1.00). Restricting the range of values (**truncating the distribution**) reduces the size of r.

One training exercise for first-grade children concentrates on the discrimination of spoken words. The child must listen to groups of three words (triads), and then make a response. Two kinds of triads are used:

Stimulus	*Response*
/can can can/	same
/ran run ran/	different

(**Auditory** stimuli will be enclosed in / /; **visual** stimuli in [ ].) If the three words are the same, the child responds "same" by circling a picture of the object or action. If the middle word is different, he circles the word *no*.

In a group of 30 first-grade children, 5 will be unable to respond to this task; of these, 2 or 3 will succeed after instruction in the use of the terms *same* and *different*. The others will require several sessions in "echoing" behavior, in which the teacher directs: "Say what I say: *ran*" and the child responds: "ran." The procedure is repeated for each word.

Another exercise is designed to teach a sounding skill for word analysis. It requires children to identify words that end alike, i.e., rhyming words, such as /pan/ and /can/. Success in this task leads to the next, responding to sounds within words. For example, "Listen for *an: pan.*"

Fewer than 20% of the second-grade children in one school system were able to discriminate the ending sounds in words dependably; 10% were successful with beginning sounds. By October of the third grade, the figures were 80% and 24% (J. M. Smith & D. E. P. Smith, 1975e).

In a third exercise, the child isolates common letter groups in words and sounds them.

For example, the child looks at the words *shoe* and *tree,* and sounds out the letter groups:

$$[shoe] = /shh\text{-}oo/$$
$$[tree] = /tur\text{-}ee/$$

Some children are able to carry the process this far without being able to identify the words. The reason is that sounding out inevitably produces sound distortions sufficient to preclude recognition of the word. Such children need training in the **recognition of distorted words**. Training exercises can be developed—but such a skill is rarely if ever formally taught.

VISUAL RECEPTIVE SKILLS

As has been the case with auditory receptive skills, the role of visual discrimination skills has been a subject of debate in the literature. Once more, an engineering paradigm can be used to establish the learner as the final arbiter.

Perhaps the most common deficiency of all in learning to read concerns discriminating similar letter forms, such as the letters [b] and [d], [p] and [q], [h] and [n] , and [t] and [f] . Data gathered on first- and second-grade children show that the deficiency persists beyond the first grade. The letter [p] , for example, was missed on a matching test by 48% of first-graders. The same item was missed by 44% of the second-graders (J. M. Smith & D. E. P. Smith, 1975e).[4]

Similarly, on a letter-naming test, [b] was misnamed by 44% of first-grade children and by 40% of second-grade children.

There are a number of skills of the same order of magnitude as those involved in letter matching. One of these is matching word endings:

asked: *asks   asked   asker*

Another is matching similar words:

what: *hat   that   wait   what*

Another, letter order:

end: *ned   den   end*

And interior letters:

people: *poeple   people   peopel   peoepl*

Fewer than 10% of second-grade children were able to match interior letters dependably. (Skill in matching letter order and order of interior letters is required primarily for spelling, rather than for reading.)

AUDITORY PRODUCTIVE SKILLS

There are basic skills in speech and language. It is evident that a child who speaks French will have trouble learning to read if all instruction is in English. It may be less evident, but no less true, that a child who speaks Black English Vernacular (BEV) will have trouble if all instruction is in Standard American English (SAE) or some vernacular other than his own. The considerable overlap between BEV and SAE tends to compound the difficulties of such children (Labov, 1969).

As demonstrated by Knudsvig (1974), the pedagogical problem yields to methods of second-language instruction using discrimination programming and auditory discrimination exercises. The child learns to speak both BEV and SAE skillfully, then learns BEV–SAE equivalents. The result is facility in translating in either direction. For example, /He in the car/ is equivalent to /He is in the car/.

Word fluency enters as a critical skill when the child begins to sound out words. On finding an unknown word in a sentence, he must generate possible words for that slot, based on syntactic and/or semantic clues and on initial

---

[4] Populations consisted of all children in the specified grades within the school system studied. The system ranks in the top quartile of Michigan districts in statewide testing.

letters. And the generation of words under various constraint conditions is eminently trainable.

VISUAL PRODUCTIVE SKILLS

Letter drawing is the first writing skill required by first-grade children. Most first-graders, however, lack a prerequisite skill, the discrimination of loci within a two-dimensional space. Given a clear writing space, the child places his pencil at some point and must aim the pencil at some nearby point—a point that does not exist. It is quite possible to train the child to hallucinate such points, i.e., to imagine a point on a blank sheet and to draw a line to that point. This tactic facilitates the drawing of letters, and pictures as well (Sommer, 1965b).

Given some minimum skill in letter drawing, children run into the problem of **standards.** Letters are too large or too small, verticals are diagonal and diagonals are horizontal, sizes of parts are unrelated, and, finally, letters are drawn backward. Asked to comment on the offending letter, children commonly say, "It's wrong." Asked what is wrong with it, they cannot say. They must first be taught a **language of letters,** terms like *straight part, curved part, toward the margin, on the base line,* and *to the top line.* After such instruction, most children are able both to describe what is wrong and to correct it before being asked.

B. Performance Deficiencies

A child's failure to perform despite adequate skill results from attentional problems. Two kinds of failures in oral reading behavior are common; each tends to be accompanied by analogous classroom behavior.

ORAL READING BEHAVIORS

Errors in oral reading tend to be preceded by erratic eye movements called **visual excursions** (D. E. P. Smith & Semmelroth, 1965). A word such as [near] will appear in peripheral vision, and the next fixation may be on the word [nest] in the line above. The excursion is accompanied by an oral error.

The simplest interpretation of this visual hyperactivity is that the reader is not under stimulus control, i.e., letters are not well discriminated. (For a different although possibly complementary position, see Goodman, 1970.) Training in letter discrimination reduces such errors substantially (Geake & D. E. P. Smith, 1961; Wiig & P. H. Smith, 1972).

A second problem in oral reading is known as **word calling.** The child sounds out each word as he meets it but fails to understand the total sentence. The first-level task, word recognition, is so difficult that the child cannot handle the second-level task, apprehension of word relationships.

The problem can be reduced or eliminated by providing tasks that require use of the context:

Circle the right word: (cat, dog)

The _____ ran up the tree.

CLASSROOM BEHAVIORS

Children who produce numerous visual excursions tend to be hyperactive, unable to focus on a task long enough to perform. Such children are not under stimulus control. "He doesn't pay attention."

Other children focus on one task to the exclusion of others. They seem to be trying to do exactly what the teacher directs—and they consistently fail to learn. They are called **passive aggressive**—i.e., they resist instruction passively while apparently following instructions to the letter, and make their teachers angry.

The techniques for handling these two problems are quite different. The first group require an unusual amount of stimulus discrimination training. The second group require feedback on their productivity. For example, a chart showing daily work output is a constant reminder to the children that their achievement is under their own control (not their teachers') and that it is deficient (D. E. P. Smith, D. Brethower, & Cabot, 1969).

C. System Factors

Even the child who is maximally ready to read may fail unless provided with the ingredients of an effective learning system: effective materials, feedback on progress, and classroom management (in the form of rule enforcement).

A series of studies carried out by myself and my associates (D. E. P. Smith, D. Brethower, & Cabot, 1969) demonstrates the effect of a deficiency in one of these factors in the system. Reading material was kept constant; feedback and rule enforcement were varied.

Figure 1.1 shows the work output of six first-grade repeaters. **Work output** is defined as the number of self-instructional tasks completed, charted cumulatively (each day's output added to that of the previous day). Sessions were of 50 minutes duration. The curves all indicate extinction of work behavior over time even though all children were successful on the tasks they attempted. They worked in a safe environment with materials they appeared to like, but they made no substantial progress—apparently as a result of inadequate (i.e., **no**) feedback.

Figure 1.2 shows the achievement of similar children who used the same materials with the same teacher but who received continuous feedback on progress in the form of points.[5] The number of tasks completed each day was

---

[5] During the first half of the sessions, children received money, 1 mill per response. In the second half, they received only points. In later studies, points (that is, information on progress) were found to be equivalent to money in motivational effect.

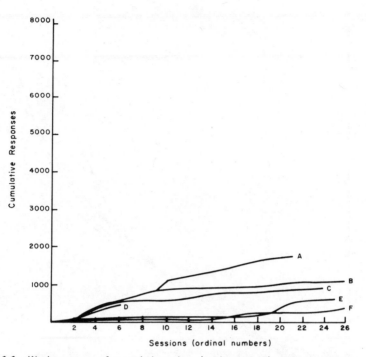

Figure 1.1. Work output of retarded readers (subjects A–F) under conditions of self-selection, self-pacing, and no feedback. Effective materials and effective management were provided. (Reprinted, with permission, from Increasing task behavior in a language arts program by providing reinforcement, by D. E. P. Smith, D. Brethower, & R. Cabot, *Journal of Experimental Child Psychology*, 1969, *8*, 45–62.)

charted on individually kept charts (not on public display). All subjects reached grade level by week 26.

Figure 1.3 shows a lesser achievement (under work contracts and praise) with rule enforcement poor or absent.

III. Some Definitions

Before we continue the explication of the learning-to-read process, a few definitions are in order.

A. *The Process*

Learning to read is a discriminative process resulting in the ordered acquisition of hierarchical responses in the visual and auditory modalities and across those modalities.

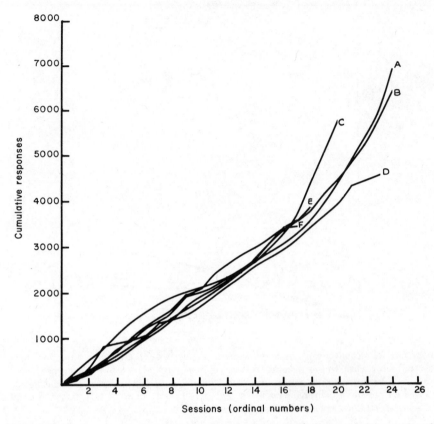

Figure 1.2. Work output of retarded readers (subjects A–F) under conditions of self-selection, self-pacing, and feedback. Effective materials and effective management were provided. (Reprinted, with permission, from Increasing task behavior in a language arts program by providing reinforcement, by D. E. P. Smith, D. Brethower, & R. Cabot, *Journal of Experimental Child Psychology*, 1969, *8*, 45–62.)

Each part of this statement will be explained briefly here and at length in ensuing chapters.

It is a discriminative process. In both vision and hearing, whole entities are discriminated from other wholes; parts are discriminated from one another within wholes; the relationships among parts are discriminated from alternative possible relationships.

It is a cross-modality process. Visual symbols are paired with auditory symbols. Graphical units (letters, words, sentences) can be made to relate isomorphically (point to point), for the most part, to utterances or to parts of them.

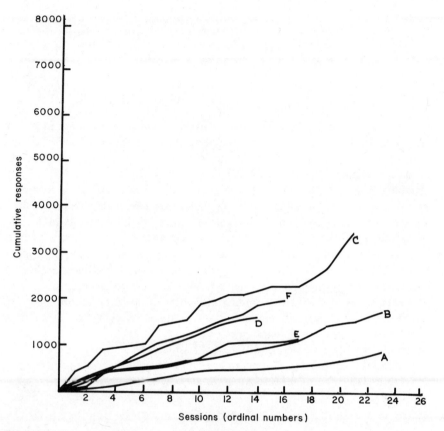

Figure 1.3. Work output of retarded readers (subjects A–F) under conditions of work contracts. Effective materials and feedback (teacher praise) were provided, but rule enforcement was poor or absent. (Reprinted, with permission, from Increasing task behavior in a language arts program by providing reinforcement, by D. E. P. Smith, D. Brethower, & R. Cabot, *Journal of Experimental Child Psychology,* 1969, *8,* 45–62.)

Responses are hierarchical. In auditory learning, for example, a developmental hierarchy may be described. First, the infant and young child respond to (and produce) the tonal patterns of utterances. Somewhat later they respond to semantic chunks (/com 'ere littleboy/), which are sometimes single words (/cookie/). Still later, they demonstrate their ability to respond to parts of words by their differential response to very similar words, as in /Give me the **truck**/ and /Give me the **duck**/, or /**Want a** cookie?/ and /**No more** cookie/. The final behavior illustrates a hierarchical nesting of discriminations made over time.

Learnings are ordered. New sets of discriminations are based on those already completed. The mastery sequence is ordered, proceeding from contours of letters upward through letters, words, sentences, and paragraphs to discourse, although the progression tends to be masked both by variations in teaching methods and by the partial independence of some skills.

B. *Language Skills*

Certain rules or principles of operation of the learning-to-read process will be put forward later. The principles are based upon a series of behavioral definitions, not necessarily widely held but necessary to this essay. Language responses consist of listening, speaking, reading, and writing.

Reading is the production of differential verbal responses under the control of visual symbols, usually words and word groups. Other symbols, like pictures and numbers, may also be read. In its simplest form, reading consists of **naming** letters and words, i.e., emitting names in the presence of those stimuli. Its more complex form, comprehension, consists of emitting questions under the control of print and transforming sentences to provide answers to those questions.

Writing is the production of visual symbols designed to produce differential verbal responses in a reader (including the writer as reader). The production is itself under the control of either a visual stimulus (copying) or an auditory stimulus (dictation or auto-dictation).

Listening is the production of differential responses to auditory stimuli.

Speaking is the production of auditory signals designed to produce differential verbal responses in a listener (including the speaker as listener).

*   *   *   *   *

The introductory section and Chapter 1 have provided two kinds of overview, one of **a** learning-to-read-and-write process, the other of **a** point of view found among some behavioral engineers. The emphasis on **a** is important. There may be a number of ways of engineering a process. Each way will develop idiosyncratic definitions and the resulting models will look somewhat different. To evaluate a model, three kinds of questions must be asked:

(*1*) Does it work? Does the "machine" produce the promised result?

(*2*) Is it internally consistent? Are the same definitions used throughout?

(*3*) What is the ratio of benefits to costs? Is there a cheaper way to get the same results?

Chapter 2 describes a way of viewing the learning process. It will be introduced by Zachary, who had a problem.

LEARNING AS A
DISCRIMINATION PROCESS

ZACHARY'S STORY

Six years old and a failure? "Really, Zack? You feel bad about being a Sparrow? Why is that?" his father asked.

"Aww," the boy replied "they're the dumb ones. The good ones are all in the Bluebirds [reading group]."

He opened his basal reader to a story. The teacher had suggested that he take the book home and practice reading it to his parents.

"Oh, this is a funny one! Listen!" he said, and began to read.

"Once—One day, Dick and Sal—Sally and Dick played a trick, uh, were playing with a ball."

"Let's play a trick on Fup—uh—Puff Sally . . ."

Dad interrupted: "Uh, Zack, try running your finger under the words."

Zack looked worried. "She don't let us do that."

"Oh," said Dad, "OK. Go ahead."

When the story was finished, Zack's father laughed convincingly, then prepared some letter-discrimination exercises. Starting with page 1 of the story, he drew the letter *a* in a box at the top of the page. He drew the letter *b* at the top of page 2, *c* on page 3, and so on. Then he counted the number of *a*'s on page 1 (there were seven of them) and wrote that number next to the letter in the box. He did this for each letter he had drawn. Then he gave the book to Zack.

"Start with page 1. Find all the *a*'s. Put a little mark under each one. There are seven of them. Then go on to page 2 and find the *b*'s."

Training exercises of this kind were continued for 10 minutes each evening. During the fourth week, Zack was promoted to the Bluebirds. In second grade, he announced that he was ahead of everybody in the "reading box" (SRA, Inc. Reading Laboratory). At the end of the third grade, his teacher recommended double promotion for Zack. The parents declined.

Zack had everything going for him—he was bright, eager, and conscientious— but he lacked one skill: accurate identification of letters. His oral reading errors were typical:

/Once/ : /One/	[Once] is a highly probable word in a story. The [c] must be noticed for a correct reading.
/Dick and Sal—Sally and Dick/	Eye sweep was too large; it reached the second name first.
/played a trick/	The next phrase to be read was [were playing]. [Played a trick] was in the line below the target line. This similarity between [playing] and [played] is a condition leading to **line slippage,** slipping to the next line.
/fup/ : /Puff/	The word has been reversed—read from right to left.

The training exercises prepared for Zack provide a sufficient condition for correcting the deficiency in most children. Running the index finger under the words is a fairly effective "crutch," i.e., a helping technique for those with letter-discrimination problems. Teachers associate use of the finger with poor reading, but they do not recognize its function. They reason incorrectly that removal of the crutch will improve the reading.

Changes in behavior attributed to learning and changes attributed to development are not qualitatively different. Such changes result from the interaction of a responsive organism and an appropriate environment.

Very little preparation of the environment is necessary for developmental change. Children grow taller and learn to walk without training, as long as basic needs are satisfied. But a richer environment is necessary for some kinds of learning. To learn a language, one needs both models to imitate and evidence of effectiveness (i.e., **feedback**). To use Skinner's term, spoken language is an **operant**, a tool for changing the environment (1957a). If mother does not jump at baby's command, if the environment is not responsive, if there is no consequence following a verbal behavior, language will not develop.

Thus, language responses may be viewed as developmental changes resulting from exposure of a responsive organism to a special environment, one in which language stimuli are both noticeable (visible) and useful. Visibility, in language instruction, is enhanced by the careful preparation and arrangement of tasks.

Presumably, any child who has intact vision and hearing, a mouth, a voice box, and a nervous system can learn to speak, and he can learn to read text materials to which he can respond aurally. All that is required is that we arrange the child's environment to that end. The first step is to determine what must be learned. This chapter will (*1*) define the things to be learned, (*2*) categorize learned responses that make a difference in the design of learning tasks, and (*3*) describe task conditions for learning.

I. Discrimination Learning

Any learning task may be construed as consisting of one or more discriminative responses. A **discriminative response is any behavior under stimulus control**, i.e., one that is more likely to occur in the presence of a given stimulus and less likely to occur in the presence of different stimuli. [As I write, the children are sledding. One is coming in the door crying. I leave my desk and go to the child to apply ice to a battered face ("bumped into a tree"). My desk-leaving behavior is under the control of the stimulus, a child's crying. A few moments later, another child comes in crying. I continue writing, allowing the child to come to me for comfort. The cry is different—in tone, loudness, in some quality ("Joey pushed me"). My desk-leaving behavior is not under the control of the second cry.] This concept of stimulus control of behavior is of fundamental importance in the construction of learning environments.

The primary task of the teacher is to arrange an environment that will allow children's behavior to come under the control of learning tasks, rather than under the control of the multifarious potential stimuli in the classroom. In the process of establishing stimulus control by learning tasks, new responses are learned. Taken together, those responses constitute the goals of instruction.

Three kinds of discriminative response can be identified: (*1*) **recognition** of a learning target, (*2*) **reproduction** of a learning target, and (*3*) **substitution** of one target for another one. And what is a learning target?

II. The Learning Target

To teachers, things to be learned include symbols to be recognized, such as words and numerals; actions to be carried out, such as talking and drawing; and relationships between symbols and actions, such as reading and writing or figuring math problems. When psychologists refer to things to be learned, they usually use the terms **stimulus (S)**, **response (R)**, and **associations** (of S and R). In this work, S's, R's and S·R's will all be referred to by the term **learning target**.

Targets consist of objects, actions, and attributes, as well as relationships among them and symbols representing them. In a learning task the thing to be learned may be a stimulus, a response, an association, or a combination of these.

Teachers often treat stimulus learnings as recognition tasks and response learnings as reproduction tasks—and thus give much practice with flash cards to produce word recognition and much practice with pencil and paper to produce printing. But learning is far more efficient when both S and R tasks are taught by means of recognition **and** reproduction.

To say that behavior is under stimulus control means that when a particular stimulus is observed, a particular response follows. The most common examples of controlling stimuli are **cues**. When I am driving the car, the red traffic light controls or cues (or signals) my stopping responses, and the green light cues my starting responses. "Dismissed" announced by the teacher cues desk- and room-leaving behavior; the teacher's frown sometimes cues immobility.

The S·R relationship involved in cueing presupposes a good deal of prior learning. A careful look at both the S (for example, the red light) and the R (car-stopping behaviors) shows that each one may be viewed as a percept that can be both recognized and reproduced.

As an image, the red traffic light has a set of features that may be **recognized**: It is round, of a certain size, usually enclosed in a rectangular box containing one or two other round shapes, and usually seen on a post at a street corner or suspended above the street at a corner. Thus, it can be recognized: The learner can make a number of discriminative responses such that a traffic light becomes a unique percept. Furthermore, as an image, it can be **reproduced**. First-grade children draw traffic lights and color them and metal workers build them. In the process of reproducing the image, the child makes a number of discriminative responses, and the result is a picture of a traffic signal. The **stimulus** is a **percept** that can be **recognized** and **reproduced**.

Is the **response** also a percept, something that can be recognized and reproduced? Stopping a car, leaving a chair, immobilizing oneself are all obviously responses. However, all can be modeled in real life or represented by pictures, and therefore may be viewed, for purposes of instruction, as percepts having stimulus characteristics that may be recognized and reproduced.

For purposes of instruction, then, the S·R relationship called **cueing** may also be described as follows: The response of recognizing a red light is followed by the response of reproducing stopping-the-car movements. From this angle we can conceptualize S's, R's and S·R's, the things to be learned, as percepts to be both recognized and reproduced.

The learning target, then, is the thing to be learned. When the task requires recognition learning (*Which one is a red light?*), the learning target or percept is obviously a stimulus requiring looking responses. But when the task requires reproduction learning (*stopping-the-car movements*), it will be learned most efficiently if the learner is first shown what stopping-the-car movements look like.

The effectiveness of this strategy was demonstrated clearly by Sommer (1965b), in a program for teaching cursive writing. Review of the literature revealed that 36% of the variance or measured difference in skill was accounted for by visual discrimination subskills and less than 3% by motor skills. (The remaining 61% was not accounted for.) In Sommer's program, discrimination tasks outnumbered production tasks by four to one. Each letter was formed by the learner only 5 to 7 times. On the other hand, training in what a correct letter form **looks like** occurred more than 25 times per letter. Naive second-grade children completed the training in 4 hours (spread over 4 weeks). The average achievement was Grade 4.2.

To recapitulate, things to be learned are learning targets—percepts to be recognized, reproduced, and associated. Once identified, the target may be analyzed systematically for instructional purposes.

A. Defining the Learning Target

A learning target is defined, first, by its points of difference from other members of its class. Thus, the letter *d* may be defined as **not** *p,* **not** *q,* **not** *b,* and **not** *a.* The confusable members of the class become the foils for teaching the unit.

The term **foil** is used rather than the more common terms, S$^\Delta$ and **non-instance.** The meaning of *foil,* in its literary usage, is "an entity whose characteristics highlight, by contrast, the critical characteristics of some focal entity." For example, a black velvet cloth is an ideal foil for a diamond because it absorbs light, whereas the diamond reflects light.

The foil controls the observing behavior of the learner.[1] If required by a forced-choice task to determine which of two figures matches a sample, the learner must locate the point of difference between the two figures. By the nature of the task, such a point of difference is a locus of high information.

---

[1] "Those features of a thing are noticed which distinguish it from other things that it is not—but not **all** the features that distinguish it from **everything** that is is not. . . . The rule is, I suggest, that only information required to identify a thing economically tends to be picked up from a complex of stimulus information [J. J. Gibson, 1966, p. 286]."

EXAMPLE.

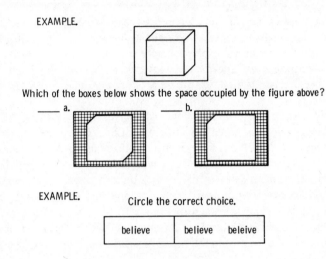

Which of the boxes below shows the space occupied by the figure above?

_____ a. _____ b.

EXAMPLE.   Circle the correct choice.

believe	believe beleive

Writers often begin a description of an entity by citing non-instances. One might say, "Let me first tell you what the 'electron cloud' theory is **not**." Similarly, the task analyst might ask this of a subject-matter expert: "What are the trainees doing wrong or failing to do under present training conditions?" Trainee errors constitute foils while trainee omissions point to areas in which foils are needed.

A target is defined, second, by identifying its parts. In a sense, identifying points of difference results in an outline of the target's structure. Identifying the components of the target leads to a definition of its internal characteristics. The components are structures serving some function in the whole. Letters and certain letter groups constitute components of a spelling word and represent certain sounds. The style of print is not a component nor is the spacing between letters, as long as each element is constant. But spacing between words is a component of a sentence to a beginning reader. Spark plugs, pistons, and fuel pump constitute parts of a gasoline engine. The steps in long division are components of the method. There may be 2 parts or 200 as in certain accounting procedures or in the predeparture checklist used by the captain of a commercial airliner.

To identify which characteristics of an entity (a structure, a process, or a method) are its component parts, one must examine other members of its class. Characteristics held in common, or **class characteristics**, are parts, as are **"unique (or distinctive) characteristics,"** which differentiate the entity from other members of its class.

A learning target is defined, third, by identifying the spatial and/or temporal relationship (the arrangement) of its parts. One might identify the placement of the loop with respect to the vertical line in *d* and *b*, the order of letters in the word *receive,* or the sequence of stages in child development. The order of parts as a necessary discrimination appears self-evident, yet is easily overlooked.

III. Kinds of Learned Responses

There are three kinds of learned responses: **recognition, reproduction,** and **substitution.** Before investigating each one in detail, I will first introduce them and give examples.

(*1*) **Recognition.** A learning target includes both stimuli and responses that are targets of instruction. The letter [d] is a stimulus and one that must be recognized and reproduced (printed or drawn) by the child. The name of that letter, /dee/, may be viewed as a response but it must also be recognized as a "word" different from /pee/ and /vee/, to be reproduced or spoken by the child. As such, it has stimulus properties to one who listens to it, including the speaker. Therefore, both stimuli and responses are viewed as targets if they are units of instruction, as described earlier.

A child recognizes a target letter when, given an array of letters, a model letter, and the direction "Find one the same as this model," he is able to match the model with the target. This is a restricted use of the word *recognize.* It does not mean "to say the name of," the more common meaning of *recognition* as used in Chapter 1. Rather, its use is limited to tasks in which some unit takes on independent existence, i.e., becomes a percept. The matching task requires the child to respond to a difference between *d* and *b,* but it does not require that the letter names be known. The closest synonym to the word recognize is *identify,* in the sense of "point to."

(*2*) **Reproduction of a stimulus** is illustrated by the child's drawing of a letter when none is in view, or saying the alphabet on request. Once more, we are not talking about naming letters: One can draw letters without being able to name them. In one study, first-grade children were asked to say the alphabet and to name all the letters in a randomly distributed array. Seventy percent were able to say the alphabet; 50% were able to name all the letters (Smith & Smith, 1975e).

Much of the school day is given over to reproducing stimuli—saying the pledge of allegiance, saying the numbers 1 to 10, singing songs, copying letters and numbers, drawing pictures. All are concerned with reproducing a visual or auditory stimulus.

(*3*) **Substitution of a stimulus,** on the other hand, takes place when the child identifies a letter or a word or a color by saying its name—or, on hearing the name, by pointing to its form. The name /dee/ is substituted for the graphic symbol [d] .

Now that we have seen one or two examples of each type of discriminative response, let us consider each one in detail.

A. *Recognition*

In recognition, a particular response occurs in the presence of a particular stimulus. To the very young infant, a face is a face is a face. He responds to any face by smiling. In time (with more experience) the infant responds to a familiar face by smiling and to an unfamiliar one by withdrawing. A small difference in a familiar face, for instance, the removal of glasses, may cause the infant to scream. The smiling response is usually described as indicating recognition. As Kagan put it, the infant "matches stimulus to schema," **schema** being defined as an "[internal] representation of an external pattern [1967, p. 136] ." As noted earlier, one learning paradigm for training children in recognition responses consists of matching exercises: The learner searches an array for the figure that matches a model figure.

A more relevant example of recognition learning is the time-honored problem of *b* and *d*. To most kindergartners, the letters *b* and *d* are equivalent. While copying the word *dad,* he may write *dab*. If told that *d* is called /dee/, he may respond to *b* by calling it /dee/. As he learns more, he discovers that *b* and *d* are different, that the placement of the loop in relation to the vertical line is a **discriminandum,**[2] a point of difference, and that the letters are not equivalent. That is something of a shock to a child since, after all, most letters when written backward remain the same letter (ʙ, ɔ, ɘ, ʇ, ʎ, etc.). When the discriminative response has occurred, we say that the child recognizes a *d*. He will take great pains to write *dad* when copying that word.

The child's action, when "he responds to any face by smiling," is commonly classified as an example of **generalization:** The child responds to mother's face by smiling and the response generalizes to other faces, the child identifies [d] as a letter in *dad* and the /d/ response generalizes to /b/.

As pointed out by Lashley and Wade (1946) and later confirmed by others (Brown, 1965; Kopp, 1965), many so-called generalization responses are errors resulting from inadequate discriminative learning. That view is followed here: To the newborn, everything is the same (i.e., equivalent); learning consists of discovering differences.[3]

---

[2] Also a **unique characteristic** or **distinctive feature.** See E. J. Gibson (1969).

[3] The Gibsons (1955, 1963, 1966, 1969) have argued this view for many years: Perceptual learning consists of responding to increasingly subtle aspects of task stimuli. "Perceptual development and perceptual learning are seen as a process of distinguishing the features of a rich input, not of enriching the data of a bare and meaningless input [J. J. Gibson, 1966, p. 320] ."

This view has important implications for education. When a child makes an error, such as confusing [b] and [d], adding 9 + 0 to get 0, calling [was] /saw/, and spelling incorrectly, we need not view him as retarded, lazy, or perceptually disturbed. He simply has yet to make certain discriminations. It is our task to arrange conditions so that such discriminations will occur. Some of those conditions are illustrated in the following discussion of reproduction learning.

B. *Reproduction*

In reproduction, a response occurs that produces a previously learned stimulus. The 2-year-old is at breakfast with the family. He says, "Want *muh.*" His mother lifts the pitcher to pour milk in his cup. He responds, in high dudgeon, "No mruk! *Muh-sin!*" She hands him a muffin and says, "Oh, a *muf-f-fin.*" He says, "Uh-huh. A *mussin.*"

The child has demonstrated recognition of muffins and of the name *muffin.* He is now learning to reproduce the name *muffin*—and, in the course of that learning, he makes imperfect attempts.

His 3-year-old sister also appreciates muffins: "Oh boy, *bearbluie* muffins!" Mother, who is wise in the ways of children's speech, says, "Blue-berry." Sister says, "Yeah, *blue-bear-y.*"

The boy has been reproducing the parts of the word *muffin;* his sister, however, has been reproducing the **order of the parts** of the word *blueberry.*

When learning to spell *receive,* the 8-year-old writes *reseve.* The 10-year-old writes *recieve,* as do many adults who have still to discriminate and to reproduce the order of the letters.

The description of language learning as a series of recognitions and reproductions (and substitutions, to be discussed next) may sound strange to the reader familiar with academic psychology. Laboratory studies usually focus on easily observable behaviors of animals, such as running or pecking. Learning is inferred from changes in rate of responding. The investigator does not often describe an animal's attempts to recognize or to reproduce a **stimulus.** But the pigeon's key-pecking behavior does result in the appearance of the desired stimulus, corn in the food tray. Hungry rats solve a maze and find food at the goal. The child says *mussin* and receives a muffin. Remember that language behavior is operant or instrumental behavior. Much of it generates stimuli to which the organism has responses.

The teacher, therefore, is concerned that the learner reproduce sounds, movements, or visual symbols that, taken together, constitute a subject matter. The learner's task is to reproduce targets—visual, auditory, and gestural. Some targets appear simple, e.g., the shape of a letter; some appear complex, e.g., a list of questions and follow-up questions contingent upon prior answers, to be asked during a medical diagnosis.

Over a series of learning trials, the learner compares his attempts with a representative or model of the target, which he has previously discriminated (recognized). He is sometimes "punished" by noting a discrepancy between his attempt and the model. He tries again, and he is rewarded by finding no discrepancy. Learning occurs. In the "mother's knee" method of teaching language, mother provides the model and, sometimes, helpful distortions (*muf-f-fins*).

C. *Substitution*

There are two kinds of substitution, one of stimuli and the other of responses.

STIMULUS SUBSTITUTION

A response to one stimulus comes to be controlled by a second stimulus. A ball constitutes a discriminative stimulus (S_1) for the spoken response /ball/ (R). Later, a second stimulus, a picture of a ball (S_2) functions as a discriminative stimulus for the response /ball/. Finally, the printed word [ball] (S_3) controls the response.

$$S_1$$
$$S_2 \cdot R_1$$
$$S_3$$

RESPONSE SUBSTITUTION

A stimulus that controls one response comes to control a second response. The command "Write an *ay*" (S) is followed by the response [ɑ], a printed letter (R_1). Later, "Write an *ay*" (S) produces [a] (R_2). Similarly, the note A played on a piano (S) produces humming of that sound (R_1), the verbal response /ay/ (R_2), or the writing of the musical notation:

The kind of analysis just described is not strictly necessary when one is concerned with developing instructional tasks. In fact, most association tasks require two-way learning:

[ball] $_S$ · /ball/ $_R$ (READING)	
The printed word [ball] elicits the spoken word /ball/.	
/ball/ $_S$ · [ball] $_R$ (WRITING)	
The spoken word /ball/ elicits the spelling of the word [ball].	

The preceding schema can be reduced to an equivalence statement:

```
[ball]    ≡    / ball /
The written and spoken words are equivalent.
```

Many formal learning tasks can be classified as substitutions or equivalents. For example, the names of things (name ≡ thing), sentence transformations, word and phrase equivalents in two languages—all are substitution learnings. (Others are mathematical proofs, creation of new visual images in drawing or painting, and creation of new auditory images in music or writing.)

Recognition and/or reproduction tasks include the discrimination of forms of letters of the alphabet; the order of letters in the alphabet; word forms; the order of words in sentences; the order of letters in words; the forms of numbers and other symbols ($<$, $>$, +); the order of numbers; sentence forms; punctuation; paragraph forms; the order of sentences in paragraphs; the parts and operation of an internal combustion engine; and the operations in arithmetic systems.

Note that these include **units** (letters, numbers, words), **structures** (words, paragraphs, engines), and **functions** (engine operation, operating methodologies in number systems).

Note also that in no case did we use the phrase *the name of* letters, words, or numbers. Actually, names too are units. But in common parlance, learning the names of objects generally implies recognizing the structure, recognizing the name, then associating name and structure. The name and the structure constitute an equivalence, a substitution learning.

We have been concerned with the three kinds of responses to be learned and the subject-matter tasks or stimuli that control them. Before turning to the conditions for learning such responses, let us look at the relationships, in particular time relationships, among the three kinds of responses.

IV. Relationships among Discriminative Responses

A. *Recognition Precedes Reproduction*

Since reproduction consists of the production of a previously learned target, recognition of a target will precede reproduction of it. Most literate adults recognize the word receive, but only a few can reproduce (i.e., spell) it.

This general rule for teaching recognition before reproduction does not deny the occurrence of a recycling stage. The 2-year-old recognizes the word *muffin,* as used by others, before he attempts to say it. Having reproduced it, after a fashion, he will make further discriminations regarding its parts, their order, its plural, and so on. Attempts to reproduce a model reveal parts of its topography not previously noticed. These parts serve as stimuli for further recognitions and reproductions.

B. Recognition and Reproduction Precede Substitution

Substitution learning assumes prior recognition of two stimuli or two responses, one to be substituted for the other. The common complaint of language teachers, "I have to teach them English grammar before they make any progress in French," reflects the requirement. If an equivalence is to be established between words or utterances of two languages or of two dialects of the same language, mastery of each term of the equivalence (English **and** French) facilitates the matching process.

Knudsvig (1974), made use of this principle in teaching black children BEV (Black English Vernacular) and SAE (Standard American English) equivalents. He taught his subjects to recognize and produce sentences in both BEV and SAE before attempting substitution training. His extremely high rate of success, 95%, is consonant with the analysis.

C. Substitution as a Special Case

The existence of three distinct types of response is largely a useful fiction. In fact, as we will see later, a substitution or paired-associate learning is produced by following the same steps as are used in training recognitions and reproductions. Three examples follow. The third is a visual–auditory pairing or substitution. The only difference is in the item to be learned—it has two elements rather than one. The target stimulus is [p] · /p/, the form of the letter and its name taken together.

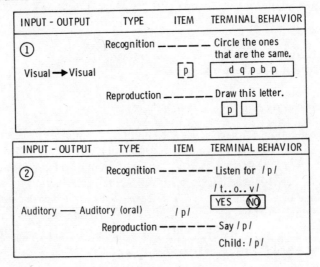

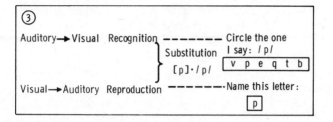

The terminal behaviors include both recognizing the letter on hearing its name (auditory input–visual output) and naming the letter (visual input–auditory (oral) output). The kinds of learning will appear from time to time in later pages, interwoven with other concepts.

V. Conditions Required for Learning Discriminative Responses

Learning occurs when conditions are arranged properly. Parents do a great deal of this arranging for the preschool child, much of it unconsciously, much of it preconsciously, very little of it self-consciously. Teachers are specialists in arranging such environments.

The well-arranged learning environment is characterized by a plethora of tasks that fulfill the proper conditions. Tasks are on paper, on tapes, on filmstrips, and in discussions conducted by a well-trained teacher.

A. Conditions for Recognition Responses

The environment includes two or more **equivalent stimuli,** i.e., one response is made in the presence of either stimulus. The child responds to both [b] and]d] by saying /d/. He responds to both [saw] and [was] by saying /was/. He responds to [6 + 3] and to [6 − 3] by saying /nine/.

Next, conditions are arranged so that **consequences are different** when the same response occurs in the presence of the two stimuli. When the child says /dee/ in the presence of [d], the teacher says "Right." When the child says /dee/ in the presence of [b], the teacher says "Wrong."[4]

It is **possible** for the learner to **respond differently** in the presence of the two stimuli. If the child can discover no difference in the physical characteristics of the letters, he must continue to respond as though they were the same. If spoken words sound the same, he will continue to respond to them similarly.

---

[4] The presence of a teacher to say "Right" and "Wrong" is not a necessary condition. The learner can use a model to generate these evaluative responses.

For example, Knudsvig (1974) reported this classroom incident: A black teacher asked her children whether /pin/ and /pen/ were same or different. They agreed that they were the same. In fact, they are the same in BEV. And the teacher was, unknowingly, speaking her home dialect.

It is possible to arrange tasks so that a discriminative response can be made. The correct and incorrect choices must differ in **one** characteristic only.

Figure 2.1 depicts two matching-to-sample tasks p/b·p (Task 1) and d/b·d (Task 2). In a tryout with a class of first-grade children, the two frames on the far left failed to meet the instructional criterion of 95% correct responses. Among 20 children, some 5 circled the wrong choice below the line in each frame. Task 1 was then revised; a reference line was added below the choices [b] and [p]. No errors occurred in the next tryout.

In Task 2, the b·d distinction failed to occur when children responded to the frame on the left. The task was revised so that the model and target were both close to the margin (middle frame). The children again failed the task. Finally, [d] and [b] were contrasted by placing them both next to the margin. That worked. The point of difference (**discriminandum** or **distinctive feature**) is illustrated on the right side of the figure.

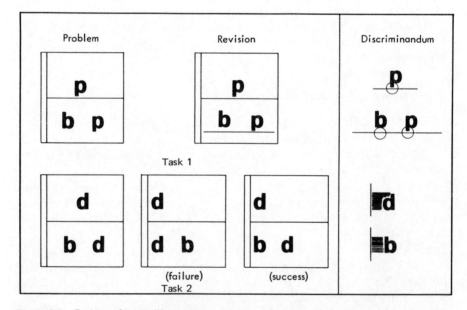

Figure 2.1. Problem frames illustrating use of an external referent (horizontal or vertical line) for initial discrimination. (Reprinted, with permission, from Learning to read as a discrimination process, by D. E. P. Smith, in D. L. Wark (Ed.), *College and adult reading*, North Central Reading Association, 1965.)

B. Conditions for Reproduction Responses

First, two or more responses occur in the presence of one discriminative stimulus. The child writes the letter *r* as [ɾ] and as [r]. He sometimes writes [receive] and sometimes [recieve]; he says /muh/ and /muh-sin/.

Next, the consequences are different when the two responses occur in the presence of the stimulus. When the child says /muh/, his mother hands him milk; when he says /muh-sin/, she hands him a muffin.

Finally, the learner discovers the critical difference between the two responses. He hears himself say /muh/ and /muh-sin/.

Given the first condition, the second and the third conditions can be created by a properly designed task:

Directions : Look at the one at the top.
Circle the one that is the same.

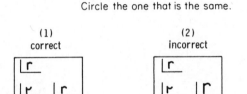

The printed *r* on the left in each frame is (linguistically) an allograph or (pedagogically) a common error. On a handwriting test following a full writing program (including the preceding frame), that usually common error did not occur among 30 heterogeneously distributed second-grade children.

The conditions of different consequences and discovery of a difference parallel the second and third conditions required for recognition learning. How then does one distinguish between recognition and reproduction learning with respect to the conditions for learning? Tasks for both deal with the learning of discriminative responses; both make use of a model, a correct choice, and an incorrect choice or foil.

The critical distinction between these two tasks is the **kind** of incorrect choice or foil used to teach the model. The foil is chosen for its contrast with some characteristic of the model. In recognition learning, the model must be discriminated from similar stimuli, primarily members of the same class: letters from other symbols; faces from other faces; words from other words. The foils then will be other letters and other symbols, other faces and other words.

In reproduction learning, on the other hand, the model must be discriminated from **incorrect variants** of itself. Thus foils are chosen from common errors, poorly drawn letters, mispronunciations, misspellings.[5]

*   *   *   *   *

[5] Further discussion of discrimination programming, paradigms, and examples is provided in Appendix A.

We have devoted a good deal of attention to synthesizing targets, to the kind of discriminative responses learners make, the order in which such responses occur, and the conditions that facilitate their occurrence. Characteristics of the learning target, such as its points of difference from similar targets, have been discussed. In Chapter 3, there will be more of the same but target stimuli will be viewed as inputs and outputs in an information-processing system.

MODALITY, LEVEL, AND SEQUENCE

BELINDA'S STORY

After Enid Huelsberg had emptied her special room, one child remained as a "special." All the others could now function in regular classrooms, but Belinda needed more resources than a brilliant teacher and a programmed curriculum. So Enid brought her to the Reading Center at The University of Michigan.

Belinda was a pleasant-appearing 9-year-old except for the vacant, slack-jawed look of the severely retarded (and of most of us when we are not processing information). Three individually administered intelligence tests given over the prior 2 years had yielded IQ scores of 52, 50, and 50. She seemed to have very little language. She was placed in a training group of six, in a corner cubicle facing the center of the room. Her training began with taped auditory-discrimination exercises.

At the end of the third 1-hour session, she came to the waiting room expecting to see her mother. She looked about wildly. Her mother was not there! The secretary said, "Belinda, your mother called. She'll be here soon."

Belinda looked at the secretary. "Momma not here . . . My momma not here." She was becoming breathless with panic. "My momma not here."

Another staff member appeared, took in the situation and said, "Belinda, your momma will be here soon."

Belinda looked at the staff member beseechingly. "Momma not here. My momma not here." Tears were forming.

At this point, the director stepped in. He had observed all the preceding events. He said, "Belinda . . . 'Linda." Belinda looked at him. She said, "Momma not here! My momma not here!" The director said, "Belinda . . . your momma's not here. Your momma's not here."

Belinda's face brightened. Then, excitedly, "Uh-huh. My momma's not here." Her voice was animated. Her statement was factual. The director's restatement had told her what she wanted to know, namely, that **she had said what she meant to say.**

The rest was anticlimactic. "She'll be here soon." Belinda had no response to that. Her nonresponse communicated all that a normal verbal child might say: "Of course she'll be here soon. She always is. So what else is new? What's really important is that I said what I intended."

*   *   *   *   *

This need for feedback by restatement is seen commonly in 3-year-olds:

Wrong		*Right*	
Child:	My tummy hurts.	*Child:*	My tummy hurts.
Parent:	It will be better after you eat.	*Parent:*	Your tummy hurts.
Child:	But my tummy hurts!	*Child:*	Un-huh. My tummy hurts.

A similar process occurs in discussions. When I disagree with a colleague, I should first restate his position, then state my own. He is much less likely to respond angrily. For after all, his first concern is that his position be understood by a rational being. (Restatement is also the cornerstone of Rogerian counseling.)

*   *   *   *   *

Raymond Cabot was directing Belinda's group. After the fourth session, he reported that she was responding randomly to the auditory training. To groups of three words such as /cake cake cake/ and /cake rake cake/, she was to respond by circling a picture of a cake if the words were the same, or by circling [no] if the middle word was different. She had received systematic training in the words *same* and *different* and in circling.

What she needed was training in echoing or miming the words. "Say *cake.*" "Cake." But we were not clever enough to recognize, at that time, this natural extension of the restatement or **single-modality feedback** requirement described in the beginning of this story. Instead we turned to another kind of feedback. We had just had a striking success by feedback of information on progress. Children had graphed the number of correct responses to programmed tasks, day by day. These "unmotivated" children had produced unbelievable amounts of work, at an accelerating rate (see Figure 1.2). The average rate per child was 250 tasks per 50-minute hour. The proportion of time spent working was 93%. One passive–aggressive boy had started at 20 tasks per hour and, by session 22, had produced 1050 tasks in one session.

So feedback on correctness of response was prescribed for Belinda. But rather than feedback at the end of 50 minutes, she was to receive feedback every 2 minutes. Richard Olds handled this training on a one-to-one basis with Belinda alone, rather than with the group. Within 2 weeks (eight sessions), Belinda had achieved a 90% level of correctness and was returned to the group. By the tenth week, her rate of work was 125 responses per 50-minute hour. (See Zeaman & House, 1967, for related work.)

Thereafter, Belinda's progress was steady. She began to converse with other children, and when that happened, her vocabulary deficiency became more apparent. About the sixtieth session, Marcia Heiman took it upon herself to develop Belinda's conversational skill. She trained Belinda's mother in shaping procedures and provided her with "scripts" to follow. Conversational skill was measured by number of sentences, length of sentence, and number of different words used.

* * * * *

At session 200 (after a total of 2 years of sessions), Belinda read at third-grade level, read for pleasure, and conversed with children and adults at a level similar to that of a dull-normal. She looked like other preadolescent girls, was well groomed, and conversed easily about her life and about the book she was now reading.

The public school placed her in their special room where she had only one problem. She was a misfit. She was the only child who could read. Her teacher solved the problem. She had Belinda read to the other children, and finally, tutor them in reading.

Much of the complexity in the learning-to-read process resides in the stimulus. i.e., in the inherent complexity of language and the symbols that represent it. But the learner himself, as processing mechanism, as receiver and producer of signals, has presented the most formidable knots to those attempting to unravel the mystery of how children learn to read.

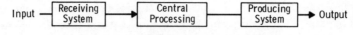

Figure 3.1. An information-processing system.

Given a single word on a page, how does the learner process it? What are the steps by which he transduces the black–white gradients of letters into electrochemical signals and, given answers to that question, what then? How does this visual pattern elicit a spoken response? And how does the spoken response relate to a written response such as spelling? These are formidable questions. But even approximate answers to any of them could lead the way to better instruction.

We can view the learner as an information-processing system, having inputs, outputs, visual receptors, auditory receptors, and a motor system. (In this discussion, outputs will be limited to recognitions and productions.) The analysis is not intended to be a definitive statement of the learning-to-read process. It is, rather, a scaffolding for erecting a learning-to-read-process, one of many possible scaffoldings for erecting one of many learning-to-read processes.

I. Single-Modality and Cross-Modality Processes

Information-processing systems have an input, a receiving system (here the sensory modalities of vision and hearing), a central processing system, a producing system, and an output. (See Figure 3.1.)

Many investigators also include a feedback loop, by means of which properties of the output are fed back to the system, modifying system operation. (See Figure 3.2.)

Let us, for the moment, collapse this self-modifying model by postponing any treatment of central processing functions. We now have a simple input–output system with feedback (see Figure 3.3), which we can apply to both single-modality and cross-modality operations.

A. *Single-Modality Processes*

The **visual** functions in learning to read and write are seeing (recognition) and drawing (reproduction). Figure 3.4 illustrates how they relate in an input–output system. We see something, draw it, and see what we have drawn, thereby

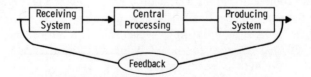

Figure 3.2. An information-processing system with feedback loop.

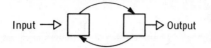

Figure 3.3. An input–output system with feedback.

allowing improvement both in seeing and in drawing. Kinesthetic (muscular) feedback is also involved, but that will be discussed later in the chapter.

The **auditory** functions, hearing (recognition) and saying (reproduction) may be represented in a similar input–output system. (See Figure 3.5.) The operation here may be described as follows: We hear something, say it, and hear what we have said, thereby allowing improvement both in hearing and in saying. (Kinesthetic feedback is also involved here.)

Single-modality systems may be described in terms of the **kinds** of inputs and outputs they include, as Figure 3.6 shows.

A visual input–output circuit includes only visual signals and an auditory circuit includes only aural signals. Seeing and drawing, hearing and saying are single-modality responses. Reading and writing, on the other hand, are cross-modality responses (also called **intersensory**).

B. Cross-Modality Processes

Graphically, it is but a small step from single- to cross-modality systems. Conceptually, that step marks the difference between animal species with and without a spoken language (however, see Premack, 1971).

Figure 3.7 shows a cross-modality input–output system. In this model, we **see and say** or **read**, and we **hear and draw** or **write**. Writing is better described, however, as **say, hear what we say, and draw**. In other words, we dictate to ourselves when we write. (Adults are generally unaware of the self-dictation, that occurs when they write, except when they spell a difficult word or when they try to compose over the shouts of children. "I can't hear myself think!") In cross-modality processes, the input–output signals now differ, as Figure 3.8 shows. Reading entails a visual input and an aural output (speaking). Writing entails an aural input and a visual output.

To summarize, for learning language skills we have available at least two parallel sensory sources, vision and hearing, for gathering information. Both

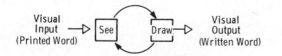

Figure 3.4. An input–output system for the single modality, vision.

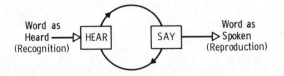

Figure 3.5. A single-modality input—output system for audition.

share a motor system that includes effector processes (eye movements, changes in posture during attending, hand and arm movements, vocal musculature).

The parallel operation of the two modalities makes it possible for one to act as a holding network while information processing (that is, attending and responding) occurs in the other. Furthermore, cycling or feedback within circuits provides for a monitoring function. Such cycling or "reverberatory activity" (Hebb, 1949) may also account for short-term memory. In vision, short-term memory is viewed as including phenomena such as visualization or imagery, visual memory and visual hallucinations. In hearing, it includes auditory rehearsal or echoic behavior, auditory memory, and auditory hallucinations.

Finally, in a primitive way, we may view the cross-modality see—say circuit as analogous to reading and the say—hear—draw circuit as analogous to writing.

II. Responses in a Cross-Modality System

Some of the relationships between kinds of responses to be learned and the input—output mechanism are summarized in Figure 3.9. The first part of the figure (I) concerns training in the learning target in the rows labeled **recognition** and **reproduction**. For example, the visual function, seeing, is trained by visual **matching** tasks, and it uses the visual—visual mode (V—V). Hearing is trained by auditory matching tasks and uses the aural—aural mode (A—A). In part II, cross-modality learning, a substitution paradigm associates stimuli by means of an identification task. Reading$_1$ is the kind of function measured by word-recognition tests. The child hears a word and circles one of three or four choices on a test form (aural→visual). Reading$_2$ is what most people mean by reading,

SENSORY MODALITY	CHANNEL	
	INPUT	OUTPUT
Vision	Visual ————→	Visual
Audition	Aural ————→	Aural (Oral)

Figure 3.6. Single-modality signals.

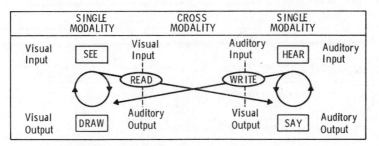

Figure 3.7. Cross-modality circuits for reading and writing.

looking at words (sentences, etc.), and, at least, saying their names (V–A). Prereading (step 3), is the last instructional step required before reading$_1$. It is illustrated in Figure 3.11. Writing, taking dictation (including auto-dictation), is what most people mean by writing.

Notice the order of learning, indicated by circled numbers. The order is congruent with the order of instructional tasks determined empirically (Smith & Smith, 1975c).

III. Objectives in a Cross-Modality System

The foregoing analysis is of limited usefulness unless it can be translated into concrete tasks. For that reason, Figure 3.9 has been transformed into a series of behavioral objectives and sample tasks (Figures 3.10 and 3.11).

In Figure 3.10, the general objectives for recognition and for reproduction are each followed by two examples, one for letters and one for contours (visual modality) and for letter names and contour names (aural modality). The tasks used here to represent instruction are selected from sequences of such tasks. They are not necessarily the first or last in such sequences. Rather, they were selected so that the similarity between objective and task would be apparent.

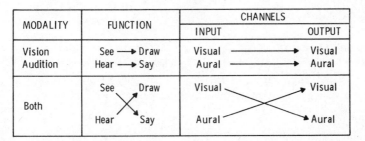

Figure 3.8. Single-modality and cross-modality input–output signals in reading and writing.

I. SINGLE-MODALITY LEARNING

RESPONSE	VISUAL		Input ⟶ Output		AURAL	
	Function	Task			Function	Task
Recognition	seeing by matching		V-V ① *	A-A ①	hearing by matching	
Reproduction	drawing by copying		V-V ②	A-A ②	saying by miming	

* Circled numbers indicate the order of learning.

II. CROSS-MODALITY LEARNING

RESPONSE	VISUAL-AURAL		Input ⟶ Output		AURAL-VISUAL	
	Function	Task			Function	Task
Recognition	pre-reading	identifying	V-A ③	A-V ④	Reading₁	identifying
Reproduction	Reading₂	oral read	V-A ⑤	A-V ⑥	Writing	taking dictation

Figure 3.9. Single-modality and cross-modality language functions and training tasks.

The format of Figure 3.11 is similar to that of Figure 3.10. The kinds of tasks differ. Both recognition (identification) and reproduction (reading and writing) include visual—aural tasks and aural—visual tasks. Once again, the sample tasks are only representative of sequences required to reach a criterion behavior.[1]

The extended schemas in Figures 3.9, 3.10, and 3.11 were provided as a bridge from the simplified model of information processing to the realities of instruction. Several kinds of tasks have been illustrated (single modality—visual matching and copying, auditory matching and miming; cross modality—various identification tasks). These do not constitute the domain of learning tasks, of course. But they were among those found to be effective for training children in the basic percepts of language. What makes this point critical is that **many other tasks were found to be ineffective.**

IV. Task Characteristics

Tasks fail to teach for many reasons: (*1*) They may assume prerequisite skills that some children do not have; (*2*) the response required may be only distantly related to the apparent task; (*3*) more than one answer may be correct; (*4*) directions may be inadequate (i.e., they may need to be taught); (*5*) too many

---

[1] For an expanded (and complete) version of the paradigm, see Figures 3.13 and 3.14 and Appendix B.

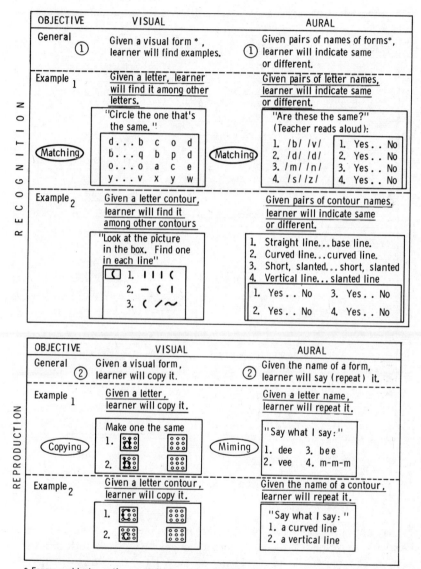

* Forms = objects, actions, attributes, symbols (letters, words, numbers, etc.).

Figure 3.10. Objectives and tasks for single-modality learning.

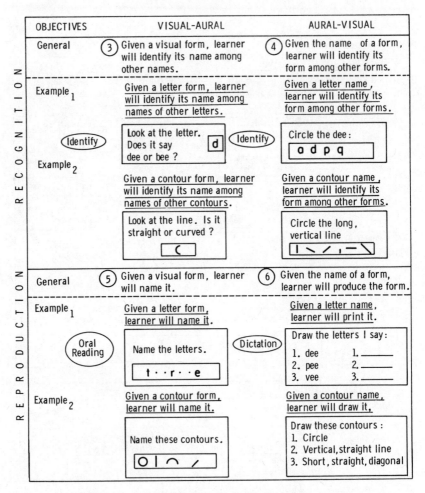

Figure 3.11. Objectives and tasks for cross-modality learning.

tasks may appear on one page; (*6*) children may be unaware of the correctness of the response until the teacher has graded them (such feedback must occur within a fraction of a second to be maximally effective); (*7*) tasks may teach answers rather than functions or processes; (*8*) tasks may be improperly ordered; and (*9*) most "teaching" tasks turn out to be "testing" tasks, in which the child knows the material or he does not. If he knows it, his learning consists of finding out that he knows something. If he does not know it, he has further evidence of his inadequacy. The task deficiencies noted in items 6, 7, and 8 merit a closer look.

FEEDBACK (ITEM 6)

There is a well-known rule of thumb in programmed learning—**the learner must have immediate feedback on the correctness of his response.** This critical concept is ordinarily implemented by presenting the correct answer to a task on the same page or on a following page (see Markle, 1969).

Certain problems arise from the use of this technique. First, inadequate tasks tend to go unnoticed by the developer since learners leave the item blank until they have looked at the key, then fill in the keyed answer. Thus, a statistical analysis tends to yield evidence of a high proportion of correct responses on inferior tasks. Second, if the learner guesses the answer and guesses incorrectly, checking the key appears to be ineffective in washing away the effects of guessing wrong (Greene, 1967). Third, the goal of instruction is not merely a right answer, but right thinking; we want the learner to carry out behaviors or sequences of behaviors that **lead to** correct answers.

An alternative to the keyed answer was modeled by Susan Markle several years ago and is now standard practice in discrimination programming. She included a model of what was to be learned in her programs, usually as a foldout at the end of the program. Whenever a learner was in doubt about his response, he was encouraged to study the model (Markle, 1968).

Model and **learning target** are names for the same concept. Models (or examples) of objects, actions, attributes, and representations are the contents of learning. Recognition, reproduction, and substitution of models or targets are the behaviors of learning.

PROCESS (ITEM 7)

Tasks that emphasize learning processes are characterized by a close control over the learner's responses. The tasks illustrated throughout this book were designed to meet the process and control criteria (for clear-cut examples, see the tasks outlined under Conditions Required for Learning Discriminative Responses in Chapter 2, those in Figures 3.9, 3.10, and 3.11, and those in the following section, Sequencing). Such control is achieved by analyzing tasks into component skills, ordering skills from lowest to highest, providing a model, and including the feedback provision **within the task.** The last requirement is the most difficult to achieve. The learner must carry out the correct processes and **know he is right when he makes his choice.** Matching-to-sample tasks provide for such knowing if two conditions are met:

Condition 1. Only two choices are included—a target, and a foil chosen to clarify a particular feature of the target.

Condition 2. Extraneous information in the task is identical for the two choices. "Extraneous" information may, in fact, not be extraneous at all. It may consist of the **ground** or background of the percept and therefore may be a necessary component. If the ground is included, it must be included for both choices.

EXAMPLE: LETTER DIRECTION

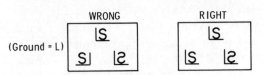

(Ground = L) WRONG   RIGHT

EXAMPLE: THE COMMA SPLICE

> *Joyce was sick and tired of housekeeping;*
> *moreover, she was unhappy with her lazy husband.*

(A) *The weapons were inappropriate for modern warfare; furthermore, the soldiers' morale was low.*

(B) *The weapons were inappropriate for modern warfare, furthermore, the soldiers' morale was low.*

(Ground = Sentence)

Each of the examples includes two choices with one point of difference. Both choices in each case are identical in background characteristics. These illustrate that matching-to-sample tasks can provide for immediate feedback if they are constructed carefully.

Another technique was devised for the perceptual-training workbook called *Visual Tracking.* (See Figure 5.6 and related discussion.) In this technique the learner is faced with a paragraph of nonsense material in which is embedded one complete alphabet. He identifies the letters, in order, under one constraint: If he misses the target letter the first time it occurs, he will not find it in the following line. Therefore, completing one line without finding a letter signals an error and the learner must begin again. His score is the total time to complete one alphabet.

A variety of clever techniques, such as chemically treated paper and mechanical devices, have been developed for providing feedback without using keys. Whether or not the materials that are used also teach processes must be determined by studying the tasks.

SEQUENCING (ITEM 8)

Within a limited domain, such as teaching a single concept, sequencing turns out to be mainly discovering the missing steps with the order determined by means of iterative development. It works as follows:

(*1*) On tryout of a series of tasks, several errors occur on one step. The task is reviewed to determine the problem. If the task can be restructured, it will be (see Figure 2.1 and text discussion). If, however, there appears to be a missing concept, new tasks must be inserted.

(*2*) A single task is developed to teach the concept. On tryout, if the new task is successful and the problem task now shows no errors, the sequence is complete. But if one or more tryout subjects still fail the problem item and also fail the new task, the new task is analyzed further.

(*3*) When the new sequence is successful and the original problem task is no longer a problem, the error has been corrected.

The final task in one sequence (Figure 3.12) caused difficulty. Several kindergarten-aged children were unable to respond despite training on *curved part, straight part,* and *margin line.* The concept *toward* was seen as the problem. To solve it, children were led from gun pointing toward, to finger (as arrow) pointing toward, to running toward, to arrow (abstraction) pointing toward, to animal facing toward, to object facing (moving) toward, to object (chair) facing toward, to circle facing toward (D. E. P. Smith & J. M. Smith, 1975b).

V. Level and Sequence

We have looked at relationships among kinds of responses to be learned (recognition, reproduction, substitution), language functions, and the kind and order of tasks leading to mastery. All these variables tend to be learner oriented.

But what about the language domain? How does one analyze the stimulus side to provide for success in learning to read? Let us here preview a later, fuller treatment of domains by positing a hierarchial sequence of units to which learners can respond:

(*1*) letter contours and contours in letters;
(*2*) letters and letters in words;
(*3*) words and words in sentences;
(*4*) sentences and sentences in paragraphs;
(*5*) paragraphs and paragraphs in discourse.

One of the many controversies in reading instruction has concerned the order of learning. Is the process learned synthetically and cumulatively by putting together letters, groups of letters, then words and sentences? Or does one start with larger units, stories or paragraphs perhaps, then build skill analytically, by identifying sentences, words, word parts, and finally, letters? Stated another way, does the best method begin with sight words and larger units, or with phonics and smaller units?

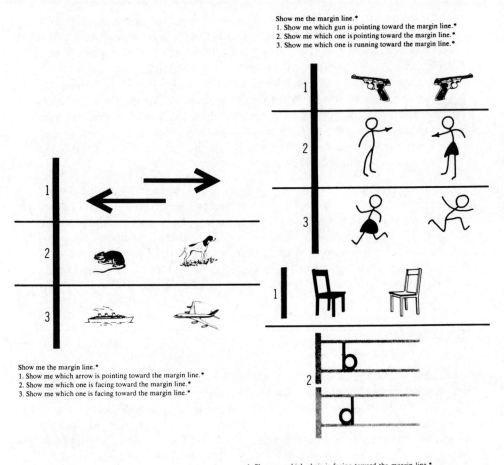

Show me the margin line.*
1. Show me which gun is pointing toward the margin line.*
2. Show me which one is pointing toward the margin line.*
3. Show me which one is running toward the margin line.*

Show me the margin line.*
1. Show me which arrow is pointing toward the margin line.*
2. Show me which one is facing toward the margin line.*
3. Show me which one is facing toward the margin line.*

1. Show me which chair is facing toward the margin line.*
2. Here are two letters. Each letter has a curved part and a straight part. Show me which one has the curved part toward the margin line.*

Figure 3.12. Sequence of discrimination tasks designed to shape use of the concept *toward.* (Reprinted, with permission, from *DIDAC,* by D. E. P. Smith & J. M. Smith. New York: Random House, Inc., 1975.)

When mastering some item, such as the name of a letter, learners use a variety of techniques. They may recite the alphabet, and comment, "That's the last letter in Amy's name," or "What's the name of that upside-down tent?" Items seem to be learned a little at a time, at several levels of complexity, with frequent regressions to apparently early levels of learning (e.g., having just succeeded in naming a *y*, the child may say, "*w, x, y, z!*").

The process is reminiscent of Gesell's principle of the "reciprocal, interweaving spiral" of growth: Any new skill, such as talking, surfaces in a primitive form, then disappears (or regresses to babbling) as another skill appears, such as walking—also in a primitive form. Then talking resurfaces in a more complex form as walking regresses to crawling (Gesell & Amatruda, 1945).

A similar pattern of development can be observed in children learning to read and write. The pattern may be described as though it consisted of **levels** (perceptual or single-modality learning and associative or cross-modality learning) and **stimuli** (contours, letters, words, etc.).

Presented in an ordered fashion, item learning follows an alternating, interlocking pathway, as shown in Figures 3.13 and 3.14. (Figure 3.14 expands the **letters** portion of Figure 3.13.)

Look at Figures 3.13 and 3.14. Consider any three juxtaposed units: contours, letters, words. Matching, copying, and miming of letter forms and names are single-modality or perceptual (P) learnings. Before letter forms are associated (A) with letter names, two other learnings take place: Contour names (A) are

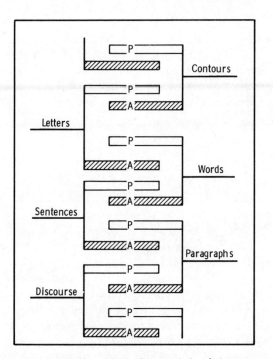

Figure 3.13. Sequence: alternating, interlocking spiral of language structures in the learning-to-read process (P represents perceptual or single-modality learning; A represents associative or cross-modality learning).

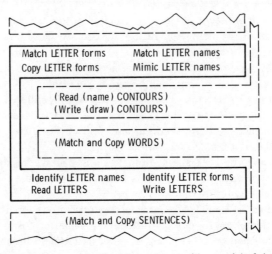

Figure 3.14. Order of learnings prescribed by an interlocking model of the learning-to-read process. (See Appendix B.)

mastered and words enter awareness at the (P) level (i.e., the percept, *word,* a group of letters beginning and ending with a space). With contours mastered and words existing as entities, two requirements of letter learning are provided for: (*1*) It can be identified by its constituent parts, e.g., circle and line; and (*2*) it can be retrieved by means of its membership in a more molar unit, e.g., [t] → /c/ /a/ /t/ → /t/.

VI. Implications of the Model

The model in Figure 3.13 appears to be congruent with both synthetic and analytic positions on the learning-to-read process. Wholes are analyzed into parts—the percept of a word is seen to consist of known letters; parts are synthesized to produce wholes—well-known letters can be put together to produce words (C. Chomsky, 1971).

If the model is a correct representation of the process, we should find that, no matter what method of teaching reading is used, synthetic or analytic, children who learn to read will master the content in the order: letters, words, sentences, and so on. That is, given some minimum essential domain of each unit, mastery should proceed as is shown in Figure 3.15.

Furthermore, we are in the enviable position of being able to agree with virtually everyone: Learning to read proceeds from whole to part—and from part to whole; one begins with the largest meaningful (associative) unit—and with the

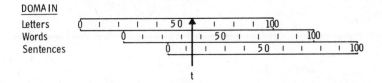

Figure 3.15 Predicted order of learnings of language units. At time *t*, for example, order of learnings for letters, words, and sentences is in the approximate ratio of 60 : 30 : 10.

smallest useful (perceptual) unit; instructional materials should be organized systematically—and children should be allowed to self-select the materials they wish to work on today (for who is to say whether the child is ready to apprehend poetry by listening to it or to draw better letters?).

This conclusion is derived partly from the logic of the interlocking model and partly from the experience of constructing a learning-to-read program. There are a number of clearly defined, well-argued positions taken by professionals in this area and there are also a number of exotic notions. My colleagues and I discovered, time and again, that alternative views tended to be correct, but at different stages of skill or relative to differing parts of the language domain. Furthermore, some of the exotic notions also turned out to be valid. Who would think, for example, that children should be trained to recognize sound-distorted words, or that word fluency can be taught, or, for that matter, that Belinda could learn to read?

* * * * *

The first three chapters have, in looking at the learning-to-read process, focused on learner capabilities and the kinds of tasks that fit the learning characteristics of children. There is also value in analyzing the reading and writing processes of mature readers. Certainly literacy concerns more than naming letters and words. What does happen when we read normally? And how do we come to develop such substantial reading vocabularies? These and related concepts will concern us in Chapter 4.

PROCESSING STIMULI

BOB'S STORY

Bob was a 22-year-old orphan. He had no memory of a family, only of home placements, none of them more than a year, all of them terminated by the foster parents on the basis of his explosiveness and incorrigibility. He entered a state home at age 8 and remained there until he was 17. At that time, he was befriended by a man who had lost his own family and who thereafter served as a father to this young boy—man. And life was good.

Bob was referred to the Reading Center for reading instruction by the personnel officer of a hospital where he worked as a messenger. His colleagues had been upset by his strange behaviors, finally interpreted by a psychologist as attempts to mask his illiteracy. He was unable to read notations such as "Rm. 330 Main Hospital E" and, unwilling to let his peers know of his deficit, he instigated conversations designed to elicit clues as to the destination. For example, Bob might say, "Look at this hellhole they're sending me to." The response elicited might be, "Hey, I'll take it. That's where that nurse is, what's-her-name, Sally Brown."

Bob was almost totally illiterate, able to write his name but unable to recognize any words on a first-grade reading test.

He drove a car but had no license. He was unable to read the driver-licensing test. His goals became those of recognizing place names required at work and qualifying for a driver's license.

By using the Fernald tracing procedure (Fernald, 1943)—our only technique for nonreaders at the time—Bob achieved his goals in 2 years. He was not yet an independent reader, but terminated meetings with us when they conflicted with baseball practice. He had begun coaching a little league team.

*   *   *   *   *

During one of our last meetings, Bob was reading a paragraph of an oral reading test. On one line were the words *from a nest long.* . . . Directly below that line appeared the words *had been reared.* Bob read the first line, as *from a near.* . . . It seemed possible that his attention had moved from *nest* to *reared,* thus eliciting *near.* Alerted to the possibility, I observed two more instances of a similar kind in the next paragraph.

If it were possible that his difficulty with reading was intensified by an inability to stay on the line, that condition would make a substantial difference to his training.

A number of attempts to measure eye movements in order to test the possibility fell short until 2 more years had elapsed. The rest of the story is told in the remainder of the chapter.

In the meantime, Bob had become an assistant scoutmaster.

Printed material to which the reader must respond may be termed the **array of stimuli** or the **stimulus array**. What are the relevant characteristics of such a stimulus array? What parts of the array control responses and how do responses occur when the array consists of a printed page? What is meant by **processing stimuli**? In order to respond to these questions we must focus on characteristics of stimuli and how stimuli are identified, on the function of the eyes during perceiving, and on the mechanics of associative learning—all necessary parts of an adequate model of the reading process.

I.   Establishing the Learning Target

We have viewed letter recognition and reproduction as an output or end product of matching tasks and of a language of letters. We shall now look more closely at characteristics of letters and words, of sounds, of visual and auditory processes, and of tasks that call these processes into play.

A. The Outcomes of Learning

As described in Chapter 2, the target, whether visual or auditory, must first be located on a ground; it must be discriminated from other forms; it must be discriminated within a larger context in which it functions as a part (e.g., a letter or a syllable in a word); its parts and the spatial or temporal relationship of the parts must be discriminated from other possible but erroneous parts and spatial or temporal relationships. Finally, its parts must be named, i.e., a language of reproduction is required.

For example, [d] is adequately defined as follows: It is not [a], not [q], not [p], not [b]; I see one in my name; it has a long, vertical line and a circle; the circle is on the baseline and toward the margin. The letter name /dee/ is not /pee/, not /bee/, not /vee/; I hear one in my name (*Sandy, a-b-c-d*); I make the name by putting my tongue in a certain place (touching the alveolar ridge).

B. Information and Response Predictability

The foregoing definition may seem unnecessarily detailed. But the reliability of occurrence of any emitted response is a function of the discriminability of the stimulus controlling that response. Ill-defined stimuli yield responses in an unpredictable way; well-defined stimuli yield responses predictably. Prior training (at the single-modality or perceptual level) in both the form and its name simplifies the associative learning step, the name–form equivalence.

Learning may be defined, for present purposes, as a reduction in the randomness of occurrence of a response. Given a particular stimulus, the more predictable the response to it is, the more complete is the learning.

A primitive or untrained system has a great deal of variability, randomness, or, technically, "information" in it, and might be pictured like this:

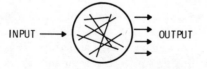

In such a system, a given input like the visual form [cat] may control a number of different outputs: /cat/, /dog/, /ate/, /I don't know/.

But, as a result of learning, the system becomes organized. Its output is quite predictable:

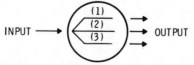

In this system, [cat] will produce (*1*) /cat/, (*2*) /c-a-t/ (i.e., /see-ay-tee/), or perhaps, (*3*) /pussy cat/ or /furry animal/, depending upon an accompanying directive: (*1*) "Say the word," (*2*) "Spell the word," or (*3*) "What does it mean?"

C. Establishing Predictable Responses to Stimuli

Information, as used here, refers to the degree of predictability of an event. Contrary to common-sense usage, information theorists refer to a random array as having more information than does a partially organized array. That is, events in a randomly organized or disorganized system are less predictable than are events in an organized system; the system thus contains more information.

Let us view the untutored child as disorganized (unpredictable) with respect to the word [cat]. Given the word [cat] to identify, he is in a **state of uncertainty**. Saying the word will be accompanied by a reduction in uncertainty. If there is no predictable, correct response to the word, the child will remain in a state of uncertainty until the stimulus changes or is removed. (An organism faced with a stimulus is said to be in a state of uncertainty. Any response followed by removal or decreased awareness of the stimulus is said to reduce uncertainty.)

A state of uncertainty is experienced as discomfort, and observers often describe the child in that state as exhibiting emotionality. Various behaviors occur, which are followed eventually by a reduction of uncertainty and a momentary experience of comfort. Those behaviors might include problem-solving attempts (focusing, saying letter names, asking questions, searching for pictures) and, in the extreme of frustration, withdrawal ("I don't know"), anger, neurotic behaviors (self-attacks, verbal attacks on others, attack of the page or book).

Whatever behavior occurs immediately prior to uncertainty reduction, whatever response is emitted immediately before the discomfort is relieved, **that response will tend to occur** in **later, similar situations**. Thus, if searching the page for a picture results in finding a picture of a cat and saying /cat/, the learner will be likely to search for a picture on the next [cat] occasion. If saying the letters /c-a-t/ (/see-ay-tee/) is followed by the response /cat/, he will be likely to say /c-a-t/ when next confronted with [cat]. Uncertainty reduction is a sufficient reinforcing condition to account for learning.

D. Task Requirements

Matching-to-sample tasks provide conditions for learning that conform to the foregoing description.

Directions: Look at the top one. Circle the one that is the same.

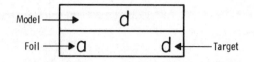

The child's uncertainty is encapsulated by the task, "Circle the one that is the same [as the top one]." He searches the two choices and discovers that they are different. One looks like the model and one does not. The point of difference is the length of the vertical line. He focuses on the target, identifies the long vertical line, and matches it to the equivalent part of the model. Uncertainty is reduced. He has learned to attend to the length of the vertical line, when faced with a [d] in a box. A long, vertical line, as contrasted with a short, vertical line or a long, slanted line, is one of several discriminanda or distinctive features of certain lowercase letters.

E. Establishing Stimulus Control of Looking and Listening

Other distinctive features of letters are line curvature, [o], completeness of curvature [c, e, n, r, t, s], relationships between lines within letters [k, f, i], and relationships of lines to a writing space [q, j, l].

Words are discriminated from the text or background as whole entities defined by white space at either end. The discriminanda here are the spaces between the words.

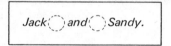

For a few first-grade children, the spaces do not function as discriminanda; they must be taught:

Directions: Look at the sentence at the top. Find one the same and circle it.

This is Jack and Sandy.
Thisis Jack and Sandy.   *This is Jack and Sandy.*

The single point of difference between target and foil is the space and lack of space between the first two words. The child notices the difference, solves the task, and begins to come under the control of or to pay attention to spaces between words.

Other points of difference between words are single letters (*boy, toy; bit, bite*) and letter order (*was, saw; on, no*).

The domain of auditory discrimination has received less attention by investigators than has visual discrimination, but it is of no less importance. Children must discriminate tonal patterns of utterances, words within utterances, words from one another, and sounds within words (phonemes, multiphoneme chunks, and syllables).

Drawing letters and writing words (reproduction) require both space-discrimination training and training in letter forms. When spelling is required, names of letters must be mastered in order to allow auto-dictation. In addition, the child must learn which letters appear in a word and the order in which the letters occur.

All these competency domains will receive attention in later chapters. For now, we can say that dependable literate behavior requires the learner's attention to be brought under the control of thousands of stimuli incorporated, for the most part, in instructional tasks.

II. Cross-Modality or Substitution Learning

Cross-modality, paired-associate learning has long been studied by psychologists, usually as a strategy for investigating characteristics of learners or of conditions for learning.[1] Given any two symbols, say the nonsense syllables *ven* and *kra*, how does one associate them such that, given /ven/ or [ven], the learner will respond with /kra/ or [kra]? The problem is similar to that faced by teachers when teaching sight words.

The **memory drum,** a laboratory version of the teacher's flash cards, has now been replaced by projection devices, automatic response-recording devices, and even payoff machines. However, until the advent of operant-conditioning techniques with their use of reinforcers and punishers, the major technique for establishing associations was repeated presentation or **repetition.** The number of repetitions or trials needed for mastery to occur has been a common measure of learning difficulty.

Whatever conditions for learning may be required, repetition of a task provides the opportunity for them to occur. But repetition of tasks has certain disadvantages in formal learning situations. For example, control of attention is even more difficult in a classroom than in a laboratory. Furthermore, irrelevant responses have an opportunity to become established, both what Skinner calls

---

[1] The following description of associative learning as a discriminative process is congruent with Gibson's position (1966, p. 272), although formulated independently—in response to the exigencies of instructional design.

superstitious behaviors (accidental contingencies) and unhealthy teacher–child interaction responses, such as dependency behaviors.

An alternative to repetition, a technique for pairing printed symbols with their names, was developed for use in the *Michigan Language Program* (D. E. P. Smith & J. M. Smith, 1975c). The procedure follows the matching-to-sample paradigm but uses complex stimuli. After discriminating [d] from [b] and [q], and /dee/ from /pee/ and /vee/, the learner discriminates the compound stimulus [d] : /dee/ from compound foils: [b] : /dee/, [d] : /bee/, and so on.

Substitution or equivalence learning is second-order learning wherein first-order learning consists of recognitions and reproductions of unitary targets. One assumes that the units to be associated (or, more accurately, for which an equivalence is to be established) are already well discriminated as single-modality learnings at the (P) level.

For example, we wish the child to look at [f] and to say /eff/ or to hear /eff/ and to draw [f]. The target stimulus is [f] ≡ /eff/ (the stimuli are equivalent: [f] = /eff/ and /eff/ = [f]). If we view this pair as the two parts of one cross-modality unit to be learned,

it can be treated as a recognition-and-reproduction task of the single-modality kind. It becomes the model. The foils then consist of all confusable *incorrect* pairings, arranged in two steps (1) discrimination and (2) recognition.

MATERIALS

Model

[f] : /eff/

Foils (V→A)		Foils (A→V)
[f] : /ee/		/eff/ : [l]
[f] : /ss/	and	/eff/ : [k]
[f] : /vee/		/eff/ : [t]

The most confusable incorrect pairings are those having one term in common with the model ([f] or /eff/) and one term incorrect (such as /ee/ or [l]). The incorrect part in each foil has been chosen for its confusability with the same-modality term in the model (e.g., [l], [k], [t]). Thus, the foils for this step are **perceptual** kinds. The left-hand foils illustrate a visual–aural input, the reading–recognition side of the cross-modality paradigm. The right-hand foils illustrate an aural–visual input, the writing–recognition side of the paradigm.

EXERCISE MODEL

(A) Discrimination

Script (taped):

Look at the letter in the box at the top. Its name is /eff/. Circle the one I say:

	┌─ Note ─┐		f
(1) /ell/	A–V foil	(1) f . . . l
(2) /eff/	A–V foil	(2) k . . . f
(3) /ee/	V–A foil	(3) e . . . f
(4) /vee/	V–A foil	(4) f . . . v
(5) /eff/	A–V foil	(5) t . . . f
(6) /ss/	V–A foil	(6) f . . . s

The foils for the recognition step are associative kinds, those already in the learner's repertoire.

(B) Recognition

(Assume that the learner knows three letters: [a] = /ay/, [b] = /bee/, [c] = /cee/.)

Look at the letter by number 1. If what I say is the name of the letter, circle the letter. If what I say is not the name of the letter, circle *No.*

(1) /ay/	(1) a . . . No
(2) /bee/	(2) f . . . No
(3) /eff/	(3) c . . . No
(4) /cee/	(4) b . . . No
(5) /eff/	(5) f . . . No
(6) /cee/	(6) c . . . No

Programming strategy specifies that the learner can return to a code-breaker, if necessary, to recall the name during the exercise. For example, prior training for this exercise included learning two responses to each of 12 words. One of these words was *fox:* [fox] = /fox/ and [fox] = /eff-oh-ex/.

The exercise model shows a two-step process: discrimination and recognition. The recognition step includes previously learned members of the letter domain. One result of using known units as foils is that new materials are discriminated from a limited domain, "things I already know," rather than from an infinite domain. These two steps constitute step 3 (prereading) in the learning sequence in Figure 3.9. A reading-recognition test (step 4) follows prereading.

To recapitulate, cross-modality pairing or equivalents are established by contrasting the pair (letter form and letter name here) with all confusable incorrect pairings. These maximally confusable pairs or foils tend to be:

Step A (1) Same form and similar-sounding name.
           (2) Same name and similar-appearing form.
Step B (3) Other form—name pairs (like *a, b, c*) already in the repertoire.

The two-step process is labeled **discrimination and recognition**. The first step may be called **forced choice** (1. *f* . . . *1* "Which one is /1/?"). The second step, called **recognition**, follows the paradigm of the true—false test (1. *a* . . . *No* "Is the name of that letter /ay/?").

The second step is a limited kind of reading-recognition test (or, strictly speaking, a letter-recognition test). Visualize the child faced with a test page having perhaps 10 items. Each item consists of three words. The teacher says one of those words. The child can select the correct choice either (1) by recognizing the word, or (2) by recognizing the **foils** and eliminating them. Our recognition test is of this second kind since foils are selected from form—name pairs already mastered.[2] (The substitution procedure described for letters and letter names was first used for teaching sight words after a number of other strategies had failed.[3])

III. Central Processing and Eye Movements

We shall now consider the letter- or word-recognition phenomenon, not from the standpoint of learning to read, but rather from the standpoint of reading. What happens when one looks at a word and recognizes it?

---

[2] For numerous examples, see Aural—visual summary units in *Reading script book*, Michigan Language Program (D. E. P. Smith & J. M. Smith, 1975c).

[3] Under tryout conditions where all prerequisite skills were assured and classroom conditions were nearly ideal, a 95% criterion for recognizing sight words was achieved. Under field conditions, 82.4% was reported (N = 16; *Standard Mastery Tasks in Language:* "Word Naming;" total possible score = 47; actual = 38.8).

A. Central Processing

An essay by Semmelroth (1965) is instructive in this regard. He first postulates that reading is information processing. After defining information as the probability of occurrence of alternative responses in the repertoire of the reader, he goes on to define **processing**.

> I have contended that alternative responses must be available for reading to occur. Our meaning of the term "information" demands that these alternatives exist at the time of the reading act. . . . I am going to argue that it is reasonable to conceive of these alternatives as relatively discrete neural circuits which may be active concurrently. Such a condition seems to be required to account for the process of visual perception. . . .
>
> There is a set of phenomena referred to as "perceptual constancies." For example, when one views a rectangular object such as a book cover from several different angles, one still sees a rectangular book cover. This is the case, even though the sensory image on the retina varies a great deal when one changes his angular relation to the book. That is, the visual image on the retina may be a parallelogram with extreme angles, and yet we "see" or perceive an ordinary rectangular book cover. Consider also some facts about the visual apparatus itself. The eye is often thought of as being analogous to a camera in its operation. The camera analogy is helpful for some purposes, but it can also be very misleading. Whereas an image can be focused clearly on the film in a camera, this is not the case in the eye. If we were able to take the retina, while the eye is fixated on some object, and develop it as we can a photographic film, the resulting picture would not begin to approach the clear, well-defined photograph of a camera. Our appreciation of the primitive state of the visual sensation is further enhanced by considering the organization of the visual receptors in the retina.
>
> The receptors themselves are not only facing *away* from the direction from which the light is coming, but they are covered by several layers of translucent cells consisting of nerve fibers and ganglion cells of several sizes and types. The picture is further complicated by their distribution. An area in the center of the visual field, smaller than the size of a penny held at arm's length, is the only place where precise pattern discriminations can be made. This area of the retina (less than 35 minutes of visual arc in diameter) contains an immense number of visual receptors (cones), but from there on out, they drop off quickly in number. Furthermore, those in the periphery must share nerve fibers so that they are less able to sense fine spatial differences in stimulation.
>
> If the eye were always perfectly stationary, only that part of the image which falls on this tiny central portion could be "seen" clearly. For this reason, it is indeed fortunate that the eyes are capable of moving with such speed and precision. But these movements themselves present a puzzling problem. That is, we perceive stable objects in the world, and yet the sensory image is jumping around from position to position on the retina.
>
> Considerations such as these lead one to a growing appreciation that the perceptual process must involve more than a simple passive identification of sensory events. The events of sensation by themselves are just not capable of accounting for the high degree of constancy, clarity and organization present in our percepts.
>
> For this reason, it is plausible to conceptualize the perceptual process as being much more "centrally" determined than a common-sense notion suggests. (The common-sense notion has the perceiver as a kind of receiver of information.) This

suggestion goes further than the so-called "new look" at perception which has come about in psychology. What is suggested here is not just that internal states such as motives or need **affect** perception. Rather, it is suggested that **previously existing** internal states of the organism **are responsible** for perception.

The concept of "information" in our model definition may now be further clarified. It has been previously identified as the amount of disorganization contained in a situation involving a number of discrete alternatives. One property which affects the amount of disorganization (information, uncertainty) is the number of alternatives present. Thus, our model of the reading process may be stated: Reading is the processing of a number of previously existing states of the organism. These states are not seen as being brought about by the presently existing sensory stimulation, i.e., the presence of the words or letters on the page, but rather they are seen as being the neural activity present while the sensory events are being initiated.

The information being processed in reading is within the person, not on the page, or on the retina. The page may be a necessary condition for this processing to take place, but it is not a sufficient condition. In order for reading to take place in terms of the present definition, **there must also be a state of uncertainty existing within the person.** Further, the processing of this uncertainty (in the presence of the print) is exactly what is meant by our definition of reading. It does not mean that **if** uncertainty is present it will be processed **when** reading takes place; rather, it says reading cannot take place unless uncertainty is present.

Now we may distinguish between two ways in which information (uncertainty) may be thought of as being "processed." If the information exists in the form of alternative internal states, these states may be most easily conceptualized as simultaneously firing neural networks. In one sense then, processing of information could refer to the "choice" of one of these networks through the interaction of sensory stimulation (looking at the word on the page) and the operation of the active networks. This process can be seen as a matching between the sensory input and the appropriate network firing. It, of course, assumes that one of the networks firing will in fact be an appropriate match for the sensory stimulation. This condition may fail to be met in either of two ways:

(1) An appropriate network may never have been formed. This would be the case when one comes across a word never seen before.

(2) The appropriate network may not be active. This would be the case when the reader's attention lapses during reading.

Thus another sense of processing may be distinguished: the initiation of firing in appropriate networks so that matching can take place. This is to be distinguished from the process of forming these networks in the first place which falls under the heading, **learning to read.**

To summarize, the definition of reading as information processing, with the appropriate specification of terms, leads us to a model of the reading process which yields several distinctions and implications.

(*1*) Reading is the processing of "uncertainty" which exists in the person, not on the page.

(*2*) This uncertainty exists (if it exists) in the form of active alternative states within the individual.

(*3*) Reading cannot take place unless these alternatives are present.

(*4*) Reading cannot take place unless these active alternatives are appropriate with respect to the material to be read.[4]

---

[4] Reprinted, with permission, from Reading as information processing, in D. L. Wark (Ed.), *College and adult reading,* North Central Reading Association, 1965, pp. 89–93.

Semmelroth goes on to suggest that coaxing a student to form questions before he or she reads a passage is actually an attempt to stimulate some uncertainty in him (1965, p. 93). I would modify that by suggesting that the uncertainty is a constant; questions encapsulate the uncertainty so that it can be reduced in the ways described.

Implicit within the foregoing analysis are the following points:

(*1*) **Alternative states** or **simultaneously firing neural networks** are the neural representations of what we have called *learning targets* (after learning has occurred).

(*2*) When an active neural network is matched by a word on the page, the motor response (name of word) is emitted, uncertainty is reduced, no further information is available in the stimulus array constituting the word, and attention shifts.

Now let us turn to the activity of the eyes while this central processing is occurring.

B. Operation of the Eyes during Reading

The usual description of eye movements during reading is as follows.

The eyes move in a coordinated or **binocular** fashion across a line of print, in a series of stops and jumps. The stop is called a **fixation** or **fixation pause**. Normal adult readers make about three fixations per line, each of about .3 seconds duration. Jumps are called **saccades.** These are ballistic movements; their direction and distance are determined at the point of origin (like a shell fired from a cannon) and are uncontrolled during "flight." The movements between fixations are incredibly swift, accounting for less than 10% of the reading time. Reading is thought to take place during the fixation since the visual threshold rises rapidly just before a movement is initiated. This rise is called **saccadic suppression** (Latour, 1962; Volkman, 1962).

There is considerable speculation about what precisely is seen during a fixation, partly because of the structure of the retina. Assuming good acuity, a clear, detailed, or sharply focused image is gained only at the **fovea** or focus point of the retina, as described by Semmelroth. During reading, the area of print equivalent to the foveal area is approximately equal to the space occupied by two adjacent letters (Taylor, 1965).

Although one does not need to see every word clearly to respond to text, it seems unlikely that three fixations per line, each focusing on two adjacent letters, would be enough to account for reading. However, these fixations tend to occur on initial letters of words, points of highest information (from the standpoint of distinguishing words from one another). It is not clear how the ballistic movement results in such accurate pinpointing, in light of the poor resolution of images across the remainder of the retina.

C. Microfixations and Micromovements

The description of visual functioning during reading leaves a number of questions unanswered, among them the amount of information processed and the control of the ballistic movements. Certain recent findings may be relevant to these problems. One characteristic of poor readers is a slow, halting delivery during oral reading, with considerable miscalling of words. Some of these errors may result from visual excursions, inaccurate movements in which the eye jumps to the line above or below or overshoots the next target word. (See Bob's Story, at the beginning of this chapter.) Similar-appearing words (or letters) in nearby words might be expected to exacerbate such errors.

While attempting to test this possibility, Smith and Semmelroth modified a device developed by Mackworth and Thomas (1962) for recording visual search behavior. The Mackworth Optiscan consists of a miniature light source, a periscope, and a movie camera. Its purpose is to record a scene as viewed by an observer (for example, a paragraph of print appearing on a screen). A small eye-position marker (a spot of light) is superimposed on the finished film to indicate where the observer is looking (fixating) from moment to moment. The image of the miniature lamp is reflected from the cornea of the left eye into the periscope and through an optical system that superimposes this marker onto the scene image. Thus the eye movements are recorded from the left eye while only the right eye is "seeing" the line of print. The finished film includes both the image of the print and the image of the marker. When the film is run, one sees the print, or paragraph, with a spot of light moving across the line as the eyes have moved across the line.

Distortions in the record are introduced by head movements and displacement of the eyeball from a constant rotational axis while reading. The authors developed a series of corrections in both the recording and analysis procedures to reduce such distortions.

A frame-by-frame analysis provided the results appearing in Figure 4.1. Line A is the record of a college student reading at a high third-grade level; line B is his record after perceptual training; line C is the record of a normal reader. Each circle has a latency of .07 seconds or less. Squares represent three or more frames too close together to allow differentiation. The following points are worthy of note:

(1) Fixations in the traditional sense (latencies of .24 to .33 seconds) consist of three or more microfixations. The slow speed of the camera (14 frames per second) makes latencies less than .07 difficult to detect. Exposure time of the film is about .03 seconds per frame. Movements within a .03-second interval are not observed except for an occasional light trace.

(2) The amplitude of micromovement within a letter ranges from 5 to 15 minutes of arc on the size of print used (the maximum visual angle subtended by an individual letter was 26 minutes of arc).

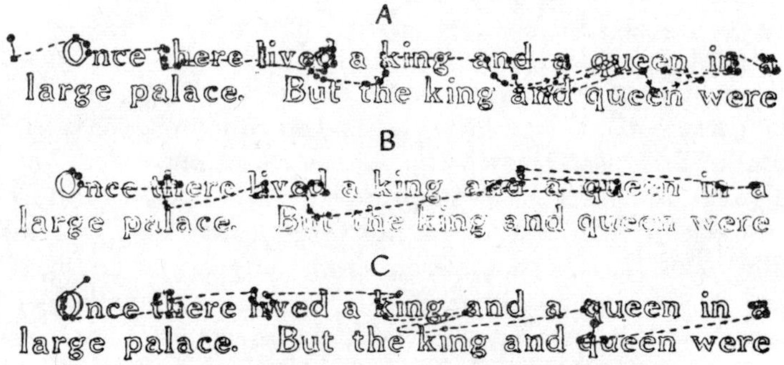

A

B

C

Figure 4.1. Micromovements of the eye during reading as recorded by a corneal-reflection technique. Circles are of .07 seconds duration or less; squares indicate three or more circles. Lines *A* and *B* are the records of a college student with a reading disability, before and after perceptual training. Line *C* is the record of a normal reader. Stimulus material consisted of solid black letters on a white field; only outlines of letters are shown here. (Reprinted, with permission, from Micro-movements during apparent fixations in reading, by D. E. P. Smith and C. Semmelroth, in D. L. Wark (Ed.), *College and adult reading*, North Central Reading Association, 1965, pp. 188–194.)

(*3*) Micromovements during a fixation appear to follow gradients forming vertical straight contours and curved ones. (Stimuli consisted of black letters on a white field.)

(*4*) Excursions occur when a similar word, letter, or identifying characteristic of a letter is adjacent to the fixated word (note *and* and *queen*).

(*5*) After perceptual training, excursions continue to occur but with less frequency and shorter latency. Total time on line A is 7.0 seconds, on Line B, 2.45 seconds.

(*6*) Excursions of extremely brief latency occur also in the record of the normal reader (total time 2.52 seconds).

The presence of microfixations and micromovements during reading may be helpful in describing visual processing. Let us consider two other developments before attempting such a description.

D. *The Effect of Stress on Perception*

Semmelroth (1963) studied the effect of stress on the size of the retinal area used during a visual estimation task. Subjects were asked to estimate the proportion of *X*'s and *O*'s apparently distributed randomly on a display board. In fact, the proportion of *X*'s to *O*'s differed systematically from the center of the board to the outside in a series of zones. Subjects fixated the center and made their estimates.

Then they were given an auditory memory task to carry out while they were estimating X's and O's. After eliminating order effects, Semmelroth found clear evidence that, under low stress (i.e., with no concomitant task involved), a narrow visual field was employed for making estimates. When the subjects were under higher stress (trying to remember a number series), an expanded visual field was used.

This finding is congruent with other "survival" information about the peripheral retina: Movement tends to be perceived most readily at the periphery; pupils tend to dilate under stress, thus allowing an increased luminance level; shapes (including word shapes) are perceived fairly accurately.

E. Control of Eye Movements

My continual references to stimulus control of attentional processes have not been accidental. Questions have been raised about the kind and amount of information transmitted by the eyes and about the control of saccaddic movements. It seems to me that answers to these questions will make a difference to the teacher as behavioral engineer. Instructional materials must be so devised that learners will respond to them in appropriate ways. What, then, does control the reader's attention?

PREDICTION

Let us assume, for the moment, that the eye moves along the black–white gradients of a letter algorithmically (in an automatic fashion). There is evidence from studies of receptors in the visual cortex of the cat that particular cells are responsive only to such gradients (Hubel & Wiesel, 1965). The series of gradients traversed and the length and direction of movements may provide a unique cortical arousal pattern. This would provide the sensory input required to match Semmelroth's alternative states or neural circuits.

But what arouses those alternative states so that they are ready to be matched by the sensory input? Numerous investigators have postulated that the reader predicts words by using syntactic and semantic constraints. Here, I would propose that there is an intervening step. As Semmelroth suggested, questions arouse uncertainty.

When such uncertainty is aroused, there is a spontaneous attempt to guess (Goodman, 1970) or predict the answer using present knowledge guided by contextual cues. Here may be the mechanism by which alternative states or schemas are aroused.

Given two possible schemas to match to one stimulus array, a printed word, the learner need only respond to the points of difference between those two schemas, or, rather, to the points of difference between the two **words**. For example,

[The big boy hit the _____ boy.]

Predictable words for that slot might be [little], [other], and possibly [bigger]. A match would be likely to occur given only one cue [l_____]. If that were the case, one fixation, at the front of the word, would accomplish the match and result in recognition. The reader has the impression that he has "seen" the whole word—as in fact he has. But most of the letters were provided by the schema, rather than by the print on the page. To say it another way, the reader hallucinated the word and the printed word did not contradict his hallucination.

SIZE OF MOVEMENT

We have described the reader when faced with a word to be recognized as being in a state of uncertainty. Presumably, a match between target and schema is equivalent to a sharp drop in information and to a concomitant sharp drop in felt uncertainty.

But this drop in uncertainty is followed immediately by a rise in uncertainty as one must predict the next word. Llewellyn Thomas (1968) has postulated a **survival reflex**, which may account for the saccade. Any novel stimulus appearing at the periphery appears to cause an automatic eye movement such that the peripheral stimulus becomes fixated foveally. When uncertainty rises precipitously, **any** stimulus other than the last word recognized will be novel. Thus we can account for a movement.

But how can we account for the **accuracy** of the movement? Recall that stress is followed by an increase in the size of the effective visual field (Semmelroth, 1963). And it has been reported by many investigators (for example, Foote & Havens, 1965) that the shape of a word tends to be perceived peripherally.

If so, we may posit a two-stage recognition process, first of shape, second of detail. It is necessary only to assume that visual schemas have shape and that they are aroused verbally given a state of uncertainty and contextual cues, so that the next schema in a sequence is ready to be matched by peripheral input. (See Gould, 1967 for related evidence.)

F. *Implications of a Stimulus-Control Model*

From an instructional-engineering point of view, the foregoing description of eye-movement control is especially useful. It suggests that visual-discrimination training should be focused on the stimuli that differentiate words, i.e., letters and sometimes letter groups, and that such distinctive features may be as finely detailed as the contours distinguishing *c* from *e, u* from *v,* or *d* from *a.* It also justifies a major emphasis on building accurate schemas, by means of discrimination training, during beginning reading instruction.

If a match is to be achieved without numerous fixations, the schemas themselves must be coded in a detailed fashion, perhaps as detailed as that achieved by the child during printing. If so, it might be helpful to the child's reading if he were to meet printing standards in the early grades.

In the verbal realm, the description places a premium on expectancies, on the prediction of next words in verbal strings, on word fluency, on alternative ways of expressing ideas (linguistically, **substitutions**) and on other aspects of meaning.

* * * * *

This chapter has concerned the physical characteristics of stimuli to be processed. It has proposed a method for producing associative learning across modalities, and has discussed the control of the eyes during reading. This task—organism interaction provides a springboard for reaching complex, higher-order processes.

Chapter 5 will describe mechanisms by which the learner may solve problems entailing those processes.

PROCESSING INFORMATION DURING READING AND WRITING

DAN'S STORY

Dan was undersized, overactive, and essentially a nonreader. He was 10 years old, in the fourth grade, and a chronic problem to his teachers, the "hyperkinetic" child. On the other hand, he was friendly and high-spirited. His mother had been declared unfit (alcoholism) and he lived with an aunt. They seemed to get along well.

As with Bob, when Dan came to us, we had no techniques for the nonreader except the Fernald tracing procedure. Here is one of several stories he wrote: *My aunt works in a restaurant. She cooks hamburgers and many other objects.*

Dan gained rapidly by using the tracing procedure and undoubtedly used other learnings picked up in school. About 2 months later (30 sessions), he was reading aloud from a Disney reader. He came to a word he did not immediately recognize [other].

"Uh-h-h, don't tell me! Uh-h-h. . . ." His eyelids began to flicker uncontrollably; his eyes looked vacant. Then, sotto voce, "My aunt cooks hamburgers and many other . . . OTHER!"

The discussion of stimulus array and eye movement in the preceding chapter focused on **observable phenomena** in the reading and writing processes. Limiting a discussion of a complex process to observables to reduce the likelihood of inventing exotic explanations has been espoused by B. F. Skinner (learning), James Gibson (perception), Kenneth Pike (linguistics), and Donald Durrell (reading). Their views have influenced this work at numerous choice points.

In this chapter, and contrary to that good advice, I wish to conjecture about what might be happening within a reader faced with an apparently simple task.

I point to the letter [a] in [cat] and say, "What's the name of that letter?"

If the first-grade child does not have an automatic answer, he tends to use information (responses) already in his repertoire to search out an answer. He may look at the letter, then at the word, say /cat/ and shake his head. Then he may look at the word again, say /see-ay-tee/, and with lifted eyebrows, respond, /ay/? In this case, he has used visual and auditory responses to the whole word[1] in the process of identifying a part. The **whole**, the word or utterance, may be viewed as a higher level—more molar—structure than the letter [a] or the sound /ay/. Faced with a stimulus and no ready response, the child moved from molecular to molar level and across modalities in his search for an answer.

	Modality		
Level	Visual		Aural
Molar	[c a t]	→	/see-ay-tee/
	↑		↓
Molecular	[a]		/ay/

How does it happen? When one faces a stimulus such as *What's the name of that letter?* or *Determine the area of a right triangle,* and no response occurs, what happens? How does one become freed from the question, from the controlling stimulus? What mechanisms arouse responses such as the visual image [cat] or the auditory image /see-ay-tee/ and what conditions are necessary to such arousal?

This chapter concerns the automatic processes that concern the foregoing questions. The reader will meet algorithms for handling recognition and reproduction responses in reading and writing. To prepare the way, we shall first specify the time frame for events.

I. The Time Frame: The Specious Present

Donald Hebb (1949) contributed a model of cortical activity that allows us to view present time as a continuum. Briefly, aggregates of nerve cells develop

---

[1] If [cat] is taught as a sight word, two responses may be taught, /cat/ and /see-ay-tee/.

interfacilitation[2] by repeated stimulation, such that a **cell assembly** is formed. When part of the assembly fires, the firing tends to be continued by using alternative pathways within the assembly, so that the life of an input is greater than the life of one nerve impulse. The firing is called **reverberatory activity**.

Many of our present-day constructs of neural events seem to be based upon the assumption that response to stimulation is more than an on–off signal; that events are anticipated; that such anticipations facilitate and even constitute perception; and that some continuing cortical activity immediately follows perceiving.

William James talked about the phenomenal experience of present time. He called it the **specious present** (1890/1950). It consists of the following:

(*1*) the immediate past, i.e., awareness of the last event preceding the present event;

(*2*) the now;

(*3*) a strong expectancy concerning what will occur in the next moment—we tend to see what we expect to see and to hear what we expect to hear. (Young child: "But you said I could go!" "I said no such thing!" "But you were about to!")

These phenomenal events, constituting present time, are shown in Table 5.1.

The "present–past" is sometimes called **iconic storage** (holding the icon or image). Although the immediate past may exist in the present visually, as an afterimage, and aurally, as an echo, the immediate future may also exist in the present, as an hallucinatory image. The matching of schema to a stimulus word may depend upon the availability of hallucinatory images.

II. Mechanisms of Information Processing

The matching of an alternative state with a stimulus cues a motor response, for example, naming of the word, and uncertainty is reduced. But let us consider a problem raised by Semmelroth: What if no alternative state exists, or none is active at this moment? The organism then exists in a state of uncertainty. It is faced with a stimulus situation to which it has no appropriate response. What then?

A. Regression and Molarity

When a state of uncertainty continues, organisms regress. Pupils of the eyes dilate, luminance increases, and features of the larger visual field become

---

[2] **Interfacilitation:** Repetitive firing tends to be followed by changes in cellular structure and relationships among cells such that pathways are formed.

Table 5.1
Events Constituting Awareness of Present Time

| | Events | | |
Modality	Present—past (retain image)	Present—present (reproduce image)	Present—future (predict image)
Visual	After image	Copy	Hallucinate
Aural	Echo	Mimic	Hallucinate

available for inspection. Concomitant with this change, and, perhaps, cued by it,[3] a more primitive, earlier-learned response occurs. In the previously mentioned example, [a] cued no response; the learner's attention moved to [cat], which cued the response /cat/. The earlier-learned response in this case is /cat/. When that response occurs, uncertainty is reduced and attention returns to [a], assuming a controlling set to name the letter.

The primitive response, then, is /cat/. But what if the question were, "What is this word?" [cat]. If the response were not available but the word had been previously studied in a larger context, the more primitive response might be that original contextual setting, *A cat drinks milk.* (Remember Dan?)

Note that in each case a more primitive, earlier-learned response tends to be a step up in molarity:

$$[A\ cat\ drinks\ milk]$$
$$\uparrow$$
$$[cat]$$
$$\uparrow$$
$$[a]$$

On the other hand, when uncertainty is reduced by making a response, there is a focusing on a more molecular stimulus if a controlling set (such as the direction "name the letter") requires it.

$$[cat] \rightarrow /see\text{-}ay\text{-}tee/$$
$$\downarrow$$
$$[a] \leftarrow /ay/$$

To summarize, when uncertainty increases, there is an increase in the probability of arousal of more primitive, more molar, earlier-learned responses. When

---

[3] That is, the size of the pupil and the portion of the retina stimulated may be related to the response initiated.

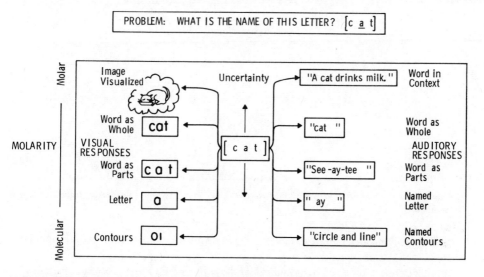

Figure 5.1. Relationship between uncertainty and molarity of response. When uncertainty rises, more-molar, earlier-learned responses tend to be aroused. A reduction of uncertainty is accompanied by focused, later-learned responses.

uncertainty decreases, there is an increase in the probability of arousal of more sophisticated, more molecular, later-learned responses.

The process is summarized in Figure 5.1. Five degrees or levels of molarity are shown with their corresponding verbal associates. Visual attention may be thought of as a kind of zoom lens, which begins with the whole word and finally focuses on single contours. In the child's reading lesson, the picture of a cat might well be included on the same page. If it is not included, the child must hallucinate such an image.

The description of events under conditions of raised and lowered uncertainty is idealized. It assumes the kind of nesting of discriminative responses earlier mentioned in auditory learning:

Image	Utterance	Word	Letter	Contours
	< A cat drinks milk.	< cat	< a	< oı

This kind of whole-to-part learning is defined in a limited way in the alternating spiral of Figure 3.13. What it implies is that the touchstone of all reading is firsthand experience, that is, at some stage, each unit mastered is a functional part of a more molar unit.[4]

---

[4] This description is not meant to negate other solutions to the identification problem. The child might regress to /apple/ or /funny circle/ or some other unmentioned response. However, since we are searching for a model on which to base instructional decisions, one explanation will suffice (if valid).

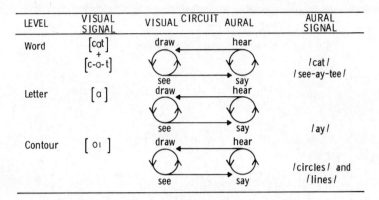

Figure 5.2. Cross-modality circuits required for analysis and synthesis (reading and writing).

The mechanism of analysis and synthesis implied here can be depicted much as the cross-modality feedback circuits of Chapter 3. Figure 5.2 shows the minimum circuitry required for analysis and synthesis; Figure 5.3 shows the movement from level to level resulting from increases and decreases in uncertainty.

The algorithm is spelled out for the question, "What is the name of this letter?" [c[a]t]. (See Figure 5.4.) The procedure makes use of the following assumption, repertoire, and rules:

Assumption Internally aroused responses are hallucinatory images and verbal predictions.

Repertoire The child has two responses to [cat]: R_1 is /cat/; R_2 is /see-ay-tee/. He has a language of letters (circles, lines, etc.).

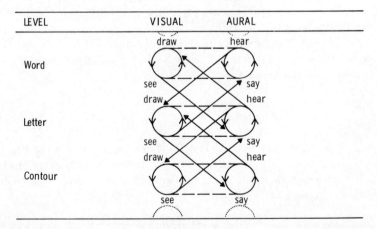

Figure 5.3. Operation of circuitry in cross-modality system to account for retrieval of response during reading and writing.

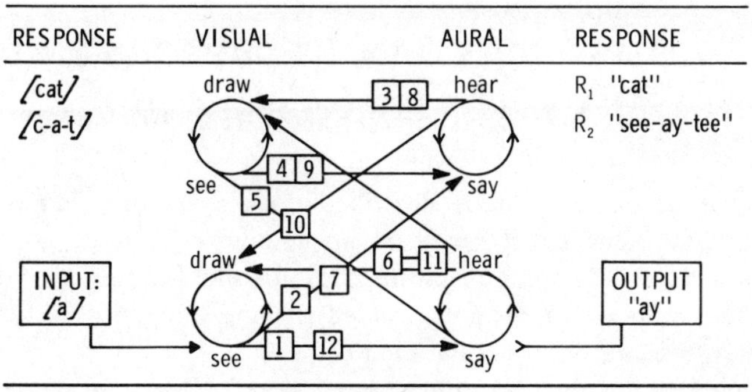

RESPONSE	VISUAL	AURAL	RESPONSE
/cat/ /c-a-t/			R₁ "cat" R₂ "see-ay-tee"

(The figure depicts a cross-modality diagram with VISUAL nodes "draw", "see" and AURAL nodes "hear", "say", connected by arrows labeled with numbered boxes 1–12, with INPUT: [a] and OUTPUT "ay" boxes.)

Stimulus	Response	Consequence
	Problem: What is the name of this letter? [a]	
(1) Input [a]	No response	Uncertainty increases. Rise one level (2)
(2) Input [a]	Say /cat/. Hear /cat/	Arouse visual response (3)
(3) [cat] : hallucinated	Predict match of /cat/ and [cat]	Arouse auditory response (4)
(4) Say /cat/	*Match*	Uncertainty decreases. Go down one level (5)
(5) Say /cat/	Predict match of /cat/ and [a]	Arouse original visual input [a] (6)
(6) Input [a]	*No match*	Uncertainty increases. Rise one level (7)
(7) Input [a]	Say /see-ay-tee/	Arouse visual response (8)
(8) [c-a-t] : hallucinated	Predict match of /see-ay-tee/ and [c a t]	Arouse auditory response (9)
(9) Say /see-ay-tee/	*Match*	Uncertainty decreases. Go down one level (10)
(10) Say /ay/	Predict match of /ay/ and [a]	Arouse visual response (11)
(11) Input [a]	*Match→Release*	
(12) Output: /ay/		

Figure 5.4. Operation of a cross-modality system to illustrate how attention might move during problem solving.

Rules   (*1*) A nonresponse is followed by synthesis, i.e., movement up-
                  ward.

                  (*2*) A match between stimulus and schema is followed by analysis,
                  i.e., movement downward.

That such an algorithm can be described does not mean that it actually operates this way. The actual processes are undoubtedly more complex and include excitation and damping of motor neurons, short-circuiting of processes, arousal of other more or less distantly related responses, bursts of motor activity described as expressions of anger, and the like.

But working out the algorithm does have a payoff. It has led to a successful procedure for teaching letter naming to beginning readers (D. E. P. Smith & J. M. Smith, 1975b). In this procedure, 12 words are taught both as sight words and spelling words. All the letters of the alphabet are represented in the group. With this "code-breaker" established, a series of tasks is given to the child. He or she is required to identify letters by calling forth both the appropriate word and its spelling. For example,

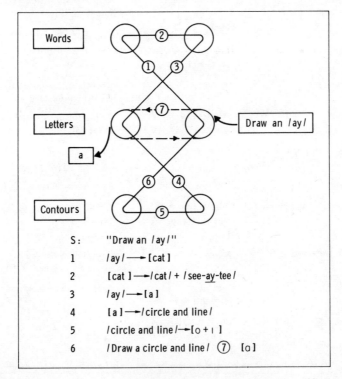

S:	"Draw an /ay/"
1	/ay/ ⟶ [cat]
2	[cat] ⟶ /cat/ + /see-ay-tee/
3	/ay/ ⟶ [a]
4	[a] ⟶ /circle and line/
5	/circle and line/ ⟶ [o + ı]
6	/Draw a circle and line/ ⑦ [o]

Figure 5.5. Problem solving in a self-dictation task, drawing a letter. Higher-level skills (spelling, sentence writing) require sentence and/or paragraph levels.

Teacher: What's this letter?   q

Child: [q]→/queen/→/cue—you . . . /→/cue/!

The most complex operation is that of self-dictation during the drawing of a letter, spelling a word, or writing an essay. A minimum of three levels is required (see Figure 5.5).

III.   Implications of a Three-Level Cross-Modality Model

I suppose there are hazards involved in **believing** that the foregoing models operate as described. But such hazards are not too dangerous. The best a model can do is to suggest alternative solutions to a concrete problem. And the worst it can do is to fail to generate solutions or to generate solutions that do not solve the problem. In that case, the model should be rebuilt or abandoned.

The present model, along with those in the early chapters, helped to resolve a number of problems faced by my colleagues and myself in the course of developing instructional materials and instructional systems. Many of these problems were concerned with establishing low-level responses or **subroutines.** A subroutine is an automatic, basic, low-level sequence of responses, upon which is built more sophisticated responses. The perceptual-level skills—attending to letters, sounds, sight words, and basic utterances; drawing legible letters; saying recognizable words; responding reliably to the phonology and syntactics of utterances and to their visual representations (function words, punctuation, transition words, etc.)—all are subroutines of reading and writing. Their importance to the final act **cannot be overstated.** If subroutines are not well defined or have gaps in them, higher-level skills requiring more of the organism's resources must be used to compensate for them.

The subroutines that concerned us in our investigation were letter discrimination, letter drawing, auditory discrimination of words, verbal fluency, naming letters, recognizing words, sounding or phonics techniques, and sentence meaning. How each problem was attacked is described next.

A.   *Letter Discrimination*

A substantial proportion of poor readers, of all ages, display problems in letter recognition as illustrated by visual excursions, miscalling of words and slow reading. In 1961, we faced the problem of developing some technique for improving letter discrimination.

Programmed learning strategies at that time tended to be response oriented.

The most obvious technique would have consisted of having learners complete incomplete letters, perhaps accentuating distinctive features.

But my colleagues were developing a stimulus-oriented strategy, which sought to (*1*) build into the learner a concept or schema of the letter by matching-to-sample tasks (as described in Chapters 2 and 3) and to (*2*) focus the learner's attention on distinctive features by selecting target and foil distinguished by only that feature (as *d* and *a, q* and *p*.)

This was a refinement of a successful strategy outlined in a book of training exercises called *Visual Tracking* (Geake & D. E. P. Smith, 1975) (first used with the college student whose eye-movement record appeared on page 72). This book consists of paragraphs of nonsense material in which the alphabet is embedded (see Figure 5.6). The learner's task is to find the letters of the alphabet, one letter at a time, in sequence.

The task is so arranged that to detect each letter the learner must discriminate it from confusable alternatives clustered near it. At least one letter appears in each line. If the learner fails to find one letter in a line, he or she is cued to an error in a preceding line. Letter size, letter spacing, and line spacing are decreased in 10 steps. The score is the time in seconds requiring to complete one paragraph. Scores are charted by the learner.

A number of effectiveness studies are described in the manual accompanying the workbook. Figure 5.7 shows the results found with 30 fourth-grade children.

```
a  b  c  d  e  f  g  h  i  j  k  l  m  n  o  p  q  r  s  t  u  v  w  x  y  z.

    Exprater otolli dohrti explmntiton. Toprxmin firggle iblix.
    Lion rtnsprs dcqeen ortif soprt ordn slj gqipr seq nvt wopn kkp.
    Iplatto risto, flittlar lib aplaptir. Nort mixi zmo iglastix.
    Wonbeas xydol. Purho ssro ip invue ttpost turj wanopbe ruy tollp.
    Frag restero ponur mort nex preppter. Claxer barb caedo kil.
    Jut timsu xge ebhij. Rra deq ernd eggspo ssw ertv ue bbpr aftree.
    Liggle beag caedi glagg. Frag ilkih caedab gead iqu kraggle sacd.
    Abln xif dho pl. Mego tni ljc fb. Ilne bko peef ubplx. Ini blc.
    Ribbi nory caedo. Iklavber ipswio aborsmer. Ljig poner boxel.
    Ceel trog ebey qol nwaeze.

                                        Min_____Sec_____
```

Figure 5.6. Sample exercise designed to train eye movement. (Reprinted, with permission, from *Visual tracking,* by R. Geake & D. E. P. Smith, 1961.)

Before training, the group's mean performance was 93 seconds to complete the task. After training, the whole group scored below the mean of their initial (pretest) performance. Twenty-three out of 30 scored at the 100th percentile of their pretest performance. The mean of the posttest scores (45 seconds) was at the 99th percentile of pretest performance. (Note that the posttraining distribution constitutes a J-curve. This curve is typical with effective training.) Similar percentage gains were reported for nine adult aphasics by Wiig and P. H. Smith (1972).

B. Letter Drawing

By 1963, we were sufficiently impressed by the results of letter-discrimination training that we began to engineer the learning-to-read process following the discrimination-learning paradigm.[5]

Early tryouts were promising. Even very primitive children could handle properly programmed tasks. However, at one point, we asked children in the first grade to respond by drawing letters. Their teacher advised us that they would not master letter drawing until the end of the school year. And this was October. Thus, we began to program letter drawing or printing.

Three complete programs were printed and discarded before the task was adequately analyzed and synthesized. Problems posed by the writing task are implicit in 7-year-old Norman's drawing of his name (Figure 5.8). At the time,

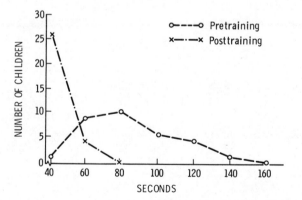

Figure 5.7. Decrease in time to complete a letter-discrimination task as a function of training in the task (*N* = 30 fourth-grade children). (From Burr, unpublished data.)

[5] The final product, *The Michigan Language Program,* was called, for a time, *The Michigan Successive Discrimination Reading Program.*

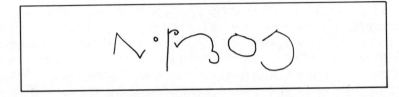

Figure 5.8. Norman's rendition of his name. (Reprinted, with permission, from Learning to read as a discrimination process, by D. E. P. Smith, in D. L. Wark (Ed.), *College and adult reading,* North Central Reading Association, 1965.)

Norman's letter discrimination (recognition) was developed to a high degree; his **reproduction** of letters was surprisingly primitive.

Norman's problem, as finally conceived, was to move his eyes from a point at which his pencil was poised to some other point on the paper. His pencil point would follow his eye movement. But there was no other point on the paper. Faced with white space, Norman had to invent or hallucinate a point to aim for. **Hallucination of points in space** might be a useful operational definition of space discrimination.

We provided Norman and his classmates with a training program to teach, first, the arrangement of points in space; then, the locus of forms in space; and finally, the imposing of forms on space. Sample frames representing nine stages are shown in Figure 5.9.

The only problem that arose during the use of this letter-drawing program was an occasional reversal error. That was handled by introducing a second-level letter-discrimination task. Whereas first-level tasks require discrimination of letters from other letters such as *a* from *d,* second-level tasks require discrimination of letters from **allographs**, incorrect variants (r : ɼ ; f : ɟ).

Sommer followed the model developed for printing in order to construct a **cursive** writing program (1965a). Children in the second semester of the second grade were used in her demonstration study. After 4 hours of instruction over 4 weeks time, the mean achievement of the demonstration group was equivalent to that of an untrained group at the beginning of fourth grade.

C. *Auditory Discrimination of Words*

Some question about the effectiveness and usefulness of auditory discrimination training has been raised in the recent literature. In 1964, we had raised similar questions. "Visual training is effective. Why not give auditory training, too?" Some members of the group asked, "Why bother? The children don't seem to need it." At that time, the only response to their argument (a perfectly

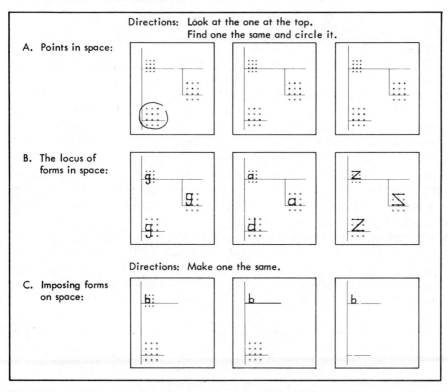

Figure 5.9. Training tasks for (A) discriminating space, (B) discriminating the locus of forms in space, and (C) imposing forms on space (writing). (Reprinted, with permission, from *Learning to read as a discrimination process*, by D. E. P. Smith, in D. L. Wark (Ed.), *College and adult reading*, North Central Reading Association, 1965.)

justified engineering argument) was a suspicion that deficits would show up in phonics tasks. In fact, we had a problem attributable to a deficit in auditory discrimination but we did not recognize the cause. Certain children appeared unable to repeat a five-word sentence. After the training program was completed, the problem disappeared.

For this program, we constructed 1200 triads of common words, 600 minimal contrastive pairs (*mice–nice–mice*) and 600 sames (*mice–mice–mice*). Each phoneme of English was contrasted with every other phoneme in the positions within words in which they normally occur. Contrasts were arranged from gross to fine and were arranged randomly with the triads of sames. The initial word of each triad was a picturable noun or verb.

Lessons of 10-minute duration were arranged. Children listened to a taped presentation; after each triad, they decided whether the words were the same or different. If the same, they circled a picture of what the word represented. If different, they circled the word *no.* The total training period was 4 weeks; 10 minutes per lesson, 5 lessons each week.

One evaluative study was reported by Cabot (1968). He constructed an auditory discrimination test with 38 pairs of words, half of them minimally contrastive (*pin* and *pen*) and half of them pairs of the same word. The children were to respond *yes* or *no,* meaning *same,* or *not same* on a response sheet, and were trained in correct responding beforehand. The same scale was administered prior to and following the training of 30 first-grade children.

Initial and final performances (pretest and posttest) are shown in Figure 5.10. Before training, half the children received chance scores, whereas 3 scored at or near 100%. After training, 2 scored average for first-graders, 5 were above average, and 23 scored at or near 100%. Mean performance was at the 90th percentile for first-graders.

The amount of improvement shown is of the order of magnitude of that found for letter discrimination. One surprising outcome of Cabot's study was the discovery of the fate of control groups. These children made gains similar to the ones receiving formal training but did so **from the beginning to the end of first grade.** Control children received only incidental classroom training. That the same kind of growth can be achieved in 4 weeks at the beginning of first grade with formal training as is achieved over the school year with incidental training is notable. One effect of the training was to bring the children under the control of the teacher's voice, i.e., teachers reported a distinct improvement in what they called **paying attention.**

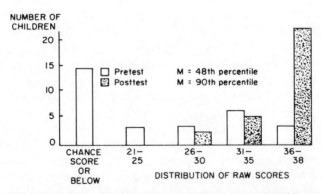

Figure 5.10. Results of training in auditory discrimination of words (Standard Mastery Task in Language, Primary I, *The Michigan Language Program,* by D. E. P. Smith & J. M. Smith, 1975c). Training time, 4 weeks. (Reprinted, with permission, from D. E. P. Smith & J. M. Smith, *The Michigan Language Program:* A case study in development. *AV Communication Review 18* (1970), 446–454.)

D. Verbal Fluency

It was much later, in 1967, that the problem of inadequate word fluency arose. In reading, when children meet a word that must be sounded out, they must generate alternative possibilities, based on context cues or on initial and/or final sounds in words. Many children make just one guess. If they are unsuccessful, they are unwilling or unable to generate more words. This constitutes inadequate word fluency.

Training in saying many words under time and sound constraints is feasible. Individual improvement curves have the general shape of learning curves. We have not collected data to demonstrate the efficacy of such training since it seems to be self-evident. In rough terms, first-grade children produce, on the average, about 10 words in 1 minute with a time constraint only (Stanford-Binet) and about 30 words after training. A systematic training program is available (D. E. P. Smith & J. M. Smith, 1975c).

The reader may be at least mildly surprised by the positive tone of the foregoing reports. You may ask, "Is it really possible to bring about such improvements in all (or nearly all) children so quickly?" The answer is "Yes, if. . . ."

The **if** refers to proper classroom conditions, which include effective materials, feedback procedures, and a willingness on the part of the teacher to have all the children succeed. If any of these conditions is lacking, training results will be less than those reported.

E. Naming Letters

Several references have been made to letter-naming procedures, especially in the section on cross-modality or substitution learning. What has not been mentioned is the series of events leading to the decision to teach letter **names** (as distinguished from letter **forms**, which were taught). By 1966, the *Michigan Language Program* was nearly completed. One of the problems that remained to be solved was teaching children to write words, that is, to spell the words they could recognize.

Related clinical work with older children had been successful. A **delayed-confirmation** procedure had been developed for extinguishing "spelling panic." But the procedure did not work with first-grade children. Direct instruction, having children do word-writing tasks with models available, was unsuccessful. We then developed programs in auditory memory (J. M. Smith, 1965) and visual memory. These did not produce spelling mastery, either.

Up to this time, it had not been necessary to teach letter names. Children were reading perfectly well without that competency. But we began to suspect that here was the difference between older and younger nonspellers. Older ones knew the names of most letters; younger tryout subjects did not. The three-level paradigm shown in Figure 5.5 specifies that the subject self-dictate letter names when spelling. But that was impossible for many of our children since they did not know the letter names.

We set about teaching letter names. The first two programs on letter naming were unsuccessful. Children learned seven or eight or nine names easily, then began to err. By now we had been attacking the spelling problem for 2 years and seemed further than ever from the goal.

At that point, we returned to the three-level model. Somehow, letter names must be stored in a higher level unit. The word [cat] stores the letters but as **sounds** rather than as **names**. Somehow the word must be used to store the letter *names*. The resolution was then simple. Teach [cat] both as /cat/ and as /see-ay-tee/. Find the smallest number of common words—picturable nouns—that include all the letters of the alphabet. Teach each as a sight word and as a spelling word. With these words in storage, any letter name can be retrieved. Thus was born *DIDAC* (D. E. P. Smith & J. M. Smith, 1975b). It produced criterion behavior and spelling mastery was consequently achieved.

F. Recognizing Words

The teaching of sight words by means of the cross-modality procedure had been achieved. But we were unwilling to have children simply recognize words. They must discriminate whole sentences, then learn the sight words within those sentences. After all, according to the three-level cross-modality model, the sentence stores the individual words for later retrieval.

To teach whole sentences, a good deal of both auditory and visual training was given. One of the exercises required matching of whole sentences (see Figure 5.11).

But some of the longer sentences ran beyond one full line so that one or two words ran over into the next line. **Some children were unable to find those words in the next line.** This came to be known as the **split-line** problem and, as it continued to defy resolution, it came to be known as the **saga** of the split line. It was finally resolved, as follows:

"Gentlemen, you are assuming that the child can be taught to read left to right and can be taught to make a return sweep. But perhaps left-to-right direction **cannot be taught** (even though it can be learned)."

"But that's absurd. If it can't be taught, how can it be learned?"

"It's learned for the simple reason that if I read [girl] from right to left, it makes no sense. If I read a sentence in the wrong direction, it makes no sense. Therefore, learning to read in the right direction requires only that the words be recognized first."

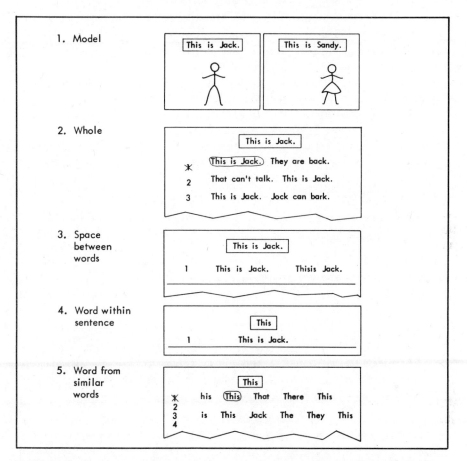

Figure 5.11. Sequence of discriminations for the visual component in the learning-to-read process. (Reprinted, with permission, from Learning to read as a discrimination process, by D. E. P. Smith, in D. L. Wark (Ed.), *College and adult reading,* North Central Reading Association, 1965.)

"But our model doesn't provide for the words to be known at this point."

"Then don't make up exercises with split lines! Once they can read the words, they'll find the ones in the next line."[6]

And so they did.

[6] The hero of this piece of trenchant reasoning was Dr. Carl Semmelroth. The colorful language of the original discussion has been modified here.

The word-analysis skills provided in the *Michigan Language Program* follow the learning of some 150 sight words. Some teachers prefer to teach word analysis (also called **word attack, sounding**) earlier in the process. They begin systematic instruction in phonics at the beginning of the first grade.

In 1969, after the *Michigan Language Program* had been completed, we began to develop a program to be used by these teachers.

Our attempts to construct a programmed phonics curriculum met with continuous frustration and failure. Nine program formats were tried. None met our criterion of 95% successful response. The first few were similar to formats now on the market. The later formats were intended to be improvements. The culmination of 6 months of frustration was a heated discussion that produced the following questions:

She: How can you get them to use *ca* when they can't get it out of storage?

He: Teach it better?

She: What's that mean? How can you teach it better?

He: Build more associations to *ca* so they can retrieve it.

She: But the program will take 3 years to get through. We have over a thousand equivalents to teach!

He: Whole to part . . . the whole for *ca* could be *cat.* Let's start with a whole word as the chunk—the analysis unit, like using *cat* to sound out *cattle.* Then teach *ca, at,* then *c, t,* and *a.* The whole, *cat,* can be retrieved easily and the parts can be reached by using the whole. You know, the three-level, cross-modality model.

It seemed to work. In the next tryout, virtually all the children were successful in the initial lessons. Visual and auditory discrimination training were included in order to reach the 95% criterion. Numerous other problems were resolved in the next 2 years. One of them deserves description here. The criterion test for one section of the program followed a four-option, multiple-choice design. The training materials, on the other hand, consisted largely of matching-to-sample items providing two choices. Since the tryout subjects had had no particular difficulty on the training materials, we were dismayed to discover a number of low scores on the criterion test.

Analysis of the relationship between training and testing materials showed a close fit, except for one difference: two options versus four options. To evaluate the possibility that the difference in number of options would account for the testing deficit, we constructed a transition exercise with three options and tried it. Sure enough, those children who scored low on the criterion test tended also to respond poorly to the **initial** items of the transition material, but to recover and respond well to the later items. Another transition exercise with four options was added and, not surprisingly, the testing deficit disappeared. We had, in effect, shaped the children to respond appropriately to four-option, multiple-choice items. The final product is a three-volume programmed phonics curriculum (J. M. Smith & D. E. P. Smith, 1975f).

H. Sentence Meaning

Problems of meaning, understanding of the stories, came up in only two instances during the 6 years of work on *The Michigan Language Program* (a first-grade curriculum). Certain precautions taken in the original scenario may have avoided other problems. All stories were based on the universal concepts described by Richards (1959) and were illustrated by stick figures—ideal for transmitting concepts.

All stories were acted out by the children to ensure understanding. The first story includes the sentence, *We are Jack and Sandy.* A boy and girl stand before the group, with joined hands, and repeat that sentence. One boy seemed unaware of the meaning of the sentence until he managed to take the hand of another child and the two repeated the sentence in unison. He broke into smiles. "Oh-h-h."

The second instance involved use of predicate nouns in conjunction with a pointing phrase, *This is. . . .* For example, *This is my mom.* The concepts were taught by contrastive pairs of pictures as shown in Figure 5.12.

A different kind of sentence-meaning problem arose with regard to directions. The directions were not those required within the program, all of which were carefully taught. Rather, the problem was in the directions given on standardized

Figure 5.12. Teaching sentence meanings with contrastive pairs of pictures. (Reprinted, with permission, from *The Michigan Language Program,* Book 3, by D. E. P. Smith & J. M. Smith. New York: Random House, Inc., 1975.)

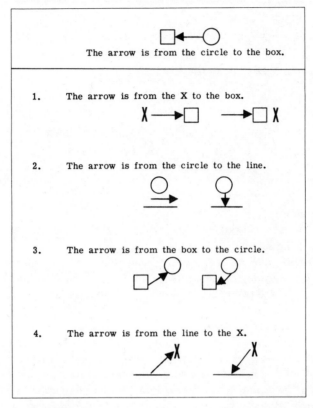

Figure 5.13. Teaching directions. (Reprinted, with permission, from Word attack and comprehension, *The Michigan Language Program,* by D. E. P. Smith & J. M. Smith. New York: Random House, 1975.)

tests. For example, "If the two things mean the same thing, put *S* on the line. If they mean different things, put *D* on the line." In the following example, I myself could not be sure whether *S* or *D* should be chosen.

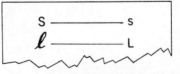

Most workbooks accompanying basal readers include directions similar to those found on standardized tests. Our tryout subjects had not had such workbooks and therefore were unfamiliar with the directions and tasks on standardized tests. Furthermore, they were used to being successful on reading and writing tasks. When faced with an unfamiliar format, they simply left the task untouched.

Because children must often take such tests and because decisions are based on the scores, we decided that the teaching of test directions was a proper activity in the program. Figure 5.13 presents a sample page.

* * * * *

This chapter has concerned algorithms for retrieving stored information while reading and writing. It describes a hierarchy of symbols (contours, letters, words, sentences, paragraphs), the top level of which is articulated with firsthand experience. Nonresponse to a symbol, according to the model, results in an increase in uncertainty and arousal of molar, synthetic responses; a decrease in uncertainty results in arousal of molecular, analytic, or focused responses.

A number of instructional design problems were resolved by using one or more of the model characteristics: letter and word discrimination, letter naming, word recognition, and phonics. Related problems in printing and following directions were also discussed.

Chapter 6 describes the domain of language competencies in reading (and writing) and specifies criterion-referenced measures.

MEASURING COMPETENCIES IN READING AND WRITING

What exactly are reading and writing skills? And how are they measured? The first step toward an adequate charting of the domain of reading has been provided by the **norm-referenced** or standardized test. The strategy for defining the domain followed by test makers for the past 50 years is as follows:

(*1*) Select two groups of children, good readers and poor readers.

(*2*) Generate test items that appear to be related to the reading task.

(*3*) Administer items to both groups, and (*a*) discard items passed by both groups, (*b*) discard items failed by both groups, (*c*) discard items passed by poor readers and failed by good readers.

(*4*) Order items from easy to difficult.

(*5*) Group items that have surface characteristics in common. Call these groups subtests.

(*6*) Repeat items 1–5 until the test is long enough to give dependable results.

(*7*) Approximate a normal distribution curve by adding and subtracting items.

(*8*) Gather data on large numbers of children and build tables of norms.

·The resulting scales are useful for ranking children with regard to one another. These items that discriminate between good and poor readers provide a **rough** charting of the domain.

A **precise** charting would require, first, that all competencies be represented in the original item pool (i.e., that all required competencies have been identified and that items exist to measure them), and second, that there be an item-selection procedure less wasteful than that just described. It is certainly conceivable that some items passed by poor readers represent component skills that they have learned; they may be poor readers because of deficits in other skills.

An adequate domain of skills can be developed. One way to accomplish this task is to define a population of primitive children and to provide whatever instruction is necessary to make competent readers of them. The validity of any instructional task can then be determined as follows:

(*1*) Child A fails a task, T_0 (terminal behavior).

(*2*) After appropriate instruction, I_0, he passes the task T_0.

(*3*) Child B fails task T_{-1} (one step removed from the terminal task).

(*4*) After instruction L_1, child B passes the task T_{-1}, receives instruction I_0, and passes T_0.

(*5*) Child C fails task T_{-2}, takes I_{-2}, I_{-1}, and I_0 and reaches T_0.

Continuation of this procedure through all the tests and all the tasks required by the most primitive child in the group will yield a series of tests representing all necessary skills. The technique unearths surprising, and not widely recognized, deficiencies in children in the areas of recognition of distorted words (auditory and visual); echoic behaviors; spacing between words; the order of letters in word interiors; the effect of set on test taking; space perception in drawing letters; the need for letter names in spelling; and word fluency.

This general strategy for defining a domain was followed in developing *The Michigan Language Program*. The course of skill acquisition inferred from that work resulted in the alternating, interlocking model of skill acquisition (Figure 3.13). A domain statement based upon that model will concern us next.

I. The Domain of Reading

The target stimuli of reading have been defined as a series of visual, aural, and cross-modality entities: contours, letters, words, sentences, paragraphs, and discourse. Two stages of learning have been described for each stimulus, a perceptual stage (P), applicable to single-modality entities, and an associative stage (A), applicable to cross-modality entities.[1]

---

[1] The associative stage (A) has been used herein to designate form–name learnings. Single-modality entities may also be associated, of course, as in uppercase, lowercase equivalents ($L = l$) and printing, cursive equivalents ($d = d$).

Two stages of learning do not adequately handle the complex functions carried out by the target stimuli of reading. For example, after the form of a word and its name are discriminated (P) and the two are associated (A), the learner may be said to have mastered a sight word. That word may now be used as a tool, first for analyzing the structures of sentences, and second for receiving and transmitting messages. Learning to use the word for analyzing structures will be termed the structural level (S). Learning to use it for receiving and transmitting messages will be termed the functional level (F).

A. Units as Structures

The child learns to recognize letters (call them by name). Next, he learns the sounds of letters and letter groups that can be used for analyzing words. The structural units within our well-worn example, [cat] = /cat/, provide a series of such letter–sound equivalents, [ca], [at], [c], [a], [t], and /ca/, /at/, /c/, /a/, and /t/. The resulting phonograms, such as [ca] ≡ /ca/, may be viewed as units with tool value. They are part of the armament used by the child in analyzing unknown words, just as words are used to analyze sentences. (Another part of the armamentarium for analyzing words consists of semantic and syntactic cues provided by phrases and sentences.)

The use of the equivalence of letters and sounds in word attack may not occur spontaneously. Instruction in using equivalents as tools is often required. Thus, we may specify, in addition to P and A, the structural level of letters and letter groups or S.

Analogous learnings at the structural level occur for contours. With appropriate instruction, letter contours may be used for identifying both letters and words (Joshua holds up two breaded shrimp, semicircular in form, and says, "Look, I can make *m* and *w* and *c* and *a*!"). Sentence syntactics may also be viewed as structural, as may certain typical characteristics of paragraphs (signal words and linkages, for example) and of discourse (the metric scheme of poetry, for example).

B. Units as Functions

In addition to the tool value of the structures of target stimuli, each kind of stimulus transmits its own kind of meaning. Words, of course, have lexical (dictionary) meaning. But single letters, such as the *s* in [bugs], carry meaning (plural) as do groups of letters (prefixes and suffixes). Even contours may be used to transmit meaning, as with the information transmitted by italics, capital letters, or heavy type in contrast to light type. In all these examples, the unit carries out a function in some larger entity of which it is a part. Instruction in those functions constitutes the fourth and top level of learning. (Some terms used to indicate function are **lexical meaning** (words), **predication type** (sentence), and **purpose** (paragraph).

The skills arranged by level and by unit appear in the matrix shown in Figure 6.1. The terms used in the matrix are approximate. In most cases, the top term is in common usage and the word below it in parentheses is recommended. For example, the skill for the unit **word** at the associative level is listed as **recognition (name)**. The term **name** (the verbal of which is **naming**) is more precise than **recognition** since the action of saying the name is implied. In a number of slots, Pike's "tagmemic" terminology is suggested because of its rigorous definitions and of the heuristic value of his framework (**K. Pike & E. Pike, 1973**).[2]

		LEVEL		
	Perceptual	*Associative*	*Structural*	*Functional*
DISCOURSE	*13°* *Universe of* *Discourse*	*18* *Précis*	*22* *Structure.* *(analysis)*	*24* *Thematic* *Interaction*
PARAGRAPH	*9* *Form*	*15* *Main Idea* *(plot)**	*20* *Structure* *(analysis)*	*23* *Purpose* *(theme* *develop.)**
SENTENCE	*A+V 6* *Boundaries** *init. capital* *end punctu.*	*11* *Intonation* *Pattern*	*17* *Syntactic* *Analysis*	*21* *Meaning* *(predication* *type)**
WORD	*A+V 4* *Shape +* *Spaces* *(boundaries)**	*8* *Recognition* *(name)*	*14* *Grammatical* *Meaning*	*19* *Lexical* *Meaning* *(term)**
LETTER	*A+V 2* *Shape*	*5* *Name*	*10* *Phonogram*	*16* *Symbols +* *Morpho-phoneme*
CONTOUR	*A+V 1* *Form*	*3* *Name*	*7* *Distinctive* *Feature*	*12* *Style of* *Print*

UNIT (row-group label at left)

Figure 6.1. Hierarchical matrix constituting the domain of reading skills. (Numbers indicate probable order of mastery; asterisks mark tagmemic terminology, after K. L. Pike & E. Pike, 1973.)

[2] Tagmemics: A linguistic theory and heuristic based on the concept of the tagmeme—a two dimensional grammatical unit with both grammatical form and grammatical meaning.

C. Sequence of Learnings

The interdependence of the skills in the matrix can be determined logically and then must be checked empirically. For example, the letter unit skill for the structural level, **phonograms** (also called **letter—sound equivalents**) has been given a value of 10 in the order of mastery. It will probably be mastered before words are used to analyze sentences (grammatical meaning—word unit, structural level—order **14**). Figure 6.1 should be viewed as a first approximation to the domain, subject to revision after better definition of terms and empirical tests.

The interdependence of skills is shown in Figure 6.2. The four levels of learning for each kind of target stimulus are represented within the interlocking pattern used in Figure 3.13. Figure 6.2 is an extrapolation of that figure. On the far left, the order of development of skills is represented by test titles. Each test title occupies a space at the same level in the hierarchy as its skill designation. For example, the first test, *Contour Matching,* is directly opposite the stimulus, *Contour Form. Letter Matching* is opposite *Letter Shape,* and so forth.

Some stimuli, such as *Style of Print* and *Distinctive Features,* are not represented by tests, since they are usually taught incidentally and are seldom tested.

The ordering of the tests follows, roughly, the order in which skills are learned. But it does not imply any particular teaching method nor the order in which skills should be taught.

This apparent paradox arises from the whole—part relationships discussed in earlier chapters. Parts are nested in wholes and wholes are parts of larger wholes. For retrieval purposes, the method of teaching should start with a whole the child can remember, possibly one- or two-sentence stories.

On the other hand, the ordering of the tests does imply the foundation skills for any given learning target. One could not expect an adequate store of sight words to be developed until *Letter Shape,* by which sight words are distinguished from one another, has been partly mastered.

Furthermore, if a child is failing to progress, the cause may be insufficient skill at underlying levels, or subroutines.

II. Criterion-Referenced Tests

Norm-referenced tests constitute a first-generation effort at defining the reading domain. **Criterion-referenced** or **mastery** tests are the second generation. Items making up criterion tests of reading and writing are operational definitions of the skills. Taken together, they constitute the goals of instruction. Instructional materials should be exactly articulated with these tests at some point.

The test names included in Figure 6.2 are meant to represent the total domain of reading. These, then, suggest the appropriate content for criterion-referenced

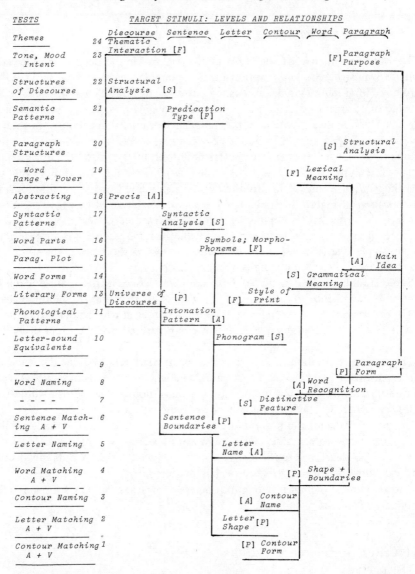

Figure 6.2. Interlocking pattern of learning targets constituting the domain of reading and resulting tests.

tests. Tests have been developed for virtually all entries and are presented fully in Volume 2 of this series.

The *Language Arts Competency Profile,* which follows on pp. 105–109, provides an outline of the tests. Five levels of skill are included, letters, words, sentences, paragraphs, and books. Each subset under the major heading provides a series of graded, one-page tests. Tests extend, in some cases, from K to 6.

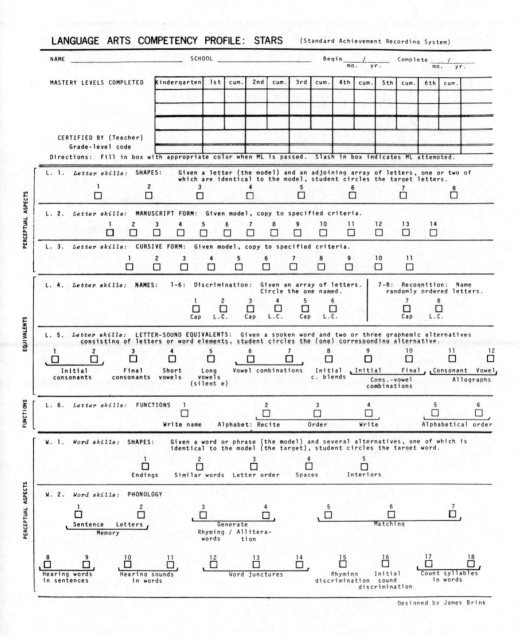

LANGUAGE ARTS COMPETENCY PROFILE: STARS (Standard Achievement Recording System)

NAME _____ SCHOOL _____ Begin ___/___ Complete ___/___
mo. yr. mo. yr.

MASTERY LEVELS COMPLETED	Kindergarten	1st	cum.	2nd	cum.	3rd	cum.	4th	cum.	5th	cum.	6th	cum.
CERTIFIED BY (Teacher)													
Grade-level code													

Directions: Fill in box with appropriate color when ML is passed. Slash in box indicates ML attempted.

PERCEPTUAL ASPECTS

L. 1. *Letter skills:* SHAPES: Given a letter (the model) and an adjoining array of letters, one or two of which are identical to the model, student circles the target letters.

1 ☐ 2 ☐ 3 ☐ 4 ☐ 5 ☐ 6 ☐ 7 ☐ 8 ☐

L. 2. *Letter skills:* MANUSCRIPT FORM: Given model, copy to specified criteria.

1 ☐ 2 ☐ 3 ☐ 4 ☐ 5 ☐ 6 ☐ 7 ☐ 8 ☐ 9 ☐ 10 ☐ 11 ☐ 12 ☐ 13 ☐ 14 ☐

L. 3. *Letter skills:* CURSIVE FORM: Given model, copy to specified criteria.

1 ☐ 2 ☐ 3 ☐ 4 ☐ 5 ☐ 6 ☐ 7 ☐ 8 ☐ 9 ☐ 10 ☐ 11 ☐

EQUIVALENTS

L. 4. *Letter skills:* NAMES: 1-6: Discrimination: Given an array of letters. Circle the one named. | 7-8: Recognition: Name randomly ordered letters.

1 ☐ 2 ☐ 3 ☐ 4 ☐ 5 ☐ 6 ☐   7 ☐ 8 ☐
Cap L.C. Cap L.C. Cap L.C.   Cap L.C.

L. 5. *Letter skills:* LETTER-SOUND EQUIVALENTS: Given a spoken word and two or three graphemic alternatives consisting of letters or word elements, student circles the (one) corresponding alternative.

1 ☐ 2 ☐ 3 ☐ 4 ☐ 5 ☐ 6 ☐ 7 ☐ 8 ☐ 9 ☐ 10 ☐ 11 ☐ 12 ☐
Initial consonants | Final consonants | Short vowels | Long vowels (silent e) | Vowel combinations | Initial c. blends | Initial Cons.-vowel combinations | Final | Consonant Vowel Allographs

FUNCTIONS

L. 6. *Letter skills:* FUNCTIONS 1 ☐ 2 ☐ 3 ☐ 4 ☐ 5 ☐ 6 ☐
Write name | Alphabet: Recite | Order | Write | Alphabetical order

PERCEPTUAL ASPECTS

W. 1. *Word skills:* SHAPES: Given a word or phrase (the model) and several alternatives, one of which is identical to the model (the target), student circles the target word.

1 ☐ 2 ☐ 3 ☐ 4 ☐ 5 ☐
Endings | Similar words | Letter order | Spaces | Interiors

W. 2. *Word skills:* PHONOLOGY

1 ☐ 2 ☐ 3 ☐ 4 ☐ 5 ☐ 6 ☐ 7 ☐
Sentence Letters | Generate Rhyming / Alliteration words | Matching
Memory

8 ☐ 9 ☐ 10 ☐ 11 ☐ 12 ☐ 13 ☐ 14 ☐ 15 ☐ 16 ☐ 17 ☐ 18 ☐
Hearing words in sentences | Hearing sounds in words | Word junctures | Rhyming discrimination | Initial sound discrimination | Count syllables in words

Designed by James Brink

LANGUAGE ARTS COMPETENCY PROFILE: STARS   (Page 2)

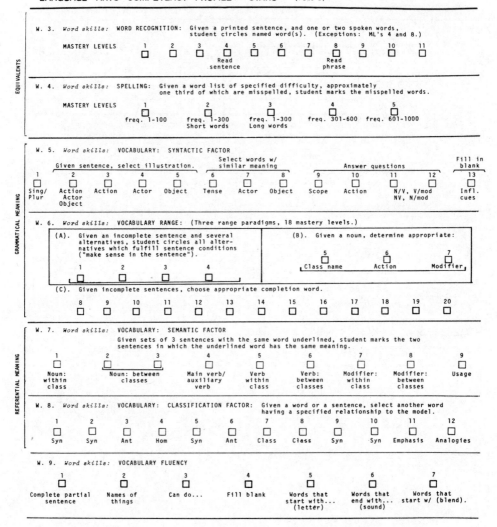

EQUIVALENTS

W. 3. *Word skills:* WORD RECOGNITION: Given a printed sentence, and one or two spoken words, student circles named word(s). (Exceptions: ML's 4 and 8.)

MASTERY LEVELS   1   2   3   4   5   6   7   8   9   10   11
                                  Read   Read
                                  sentence   phrase

W. 4. *Word skills:* SPELLING: Given a word list of specified difficulty, approximately one third of which are misspelled, student marks the misspelled words.

MASTERY LEVELS   1   2   3   4   5
                   freq. 1-100   freq. 1-300   freq. 1-300   freq. 301-600 freq. 601-1000
                                  Short words   Long words

GRAMMATICAL MEANING

W. 5. *Word skills:* VOCABULARY: SYNTACTIC FACTOR

                                                    Select words w/   Fill in
              Given sentence, select illustration. similar meaning   Answer questions   blank
   1   2   3   4   5   6   7   8   9   10   11   12   13
Sing/ Action Action Actor Object Tense Actor Object Scope Action N/V,   Infl.
Plur   Actor   V/mod cues
       Object   NV, N/mod

W. 6. *Word skills:* VOCABULARY RANGE: (Three range paradigms, 18 mastery levels.)

(A). Given an incomplete sentence and several   (B). Given a noun, determine appropriate:
      alternatives, student circles all alter-
      natives which fulfill sentence conditions   5   6   7
      ("make sense in the sentence").   Class name   Action   Modifier

          1   2   3   4

(C). Given incomplete sentences, choose appropriate completion word.

   8   9   10   11   12   13   14   15   16   17   18   19   20

REFERENTIAL MEANING

W. 7. *Word skills:* VOCABULARY: SEMANTIC FACTOR

         Given sets of 3 sentences with the same word underlined, student marks the two
         sentences in which the underlined word has the same meaning.

   1   2   3   4   5   6   7   8   9
Noun: Noun: between   Main verb/ Verb   Verb: Modifier: Modifier: Usage
within   classes   auxiliary   within   between   within   between
class   verb   class   classes   class   classes

W. 8. *Word skills:* VOCABULARY: CLASSIFICATION FACTOR: Given a word or a sentence, select another word
                                           having a specified relationship to the model.

   1   2   3   4   5   6   7   8   9   10   11   12
 Syn Syn Ant Hom Syn Ant Class Class Syn Syn Emphasis Analogies

W. 9. *Word skills:* VOCABULARY FLUENCY

        1   2   3   4   5   6   7
Complete partial Names of Can do... Fill blank Words that Words that Words that
sentence   things   start with...end with... start w/ (blend).
                                                (letter)   (sound)

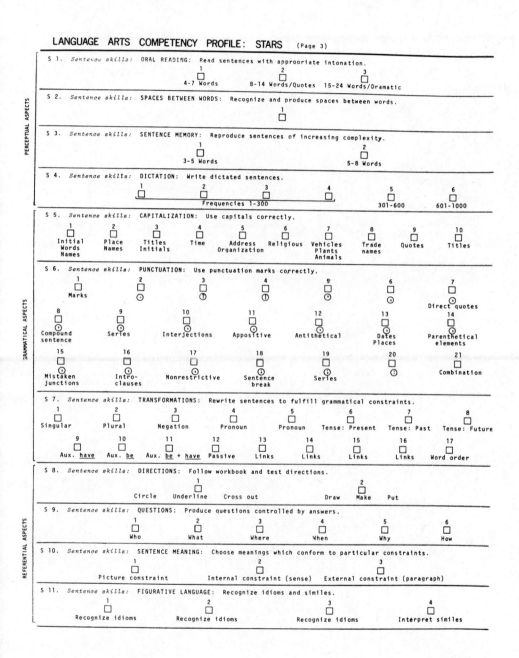

LANGUAGE ARTS COMPETENCY PROFILE: STARS (Page 3)

PERCEPTUAL ASPECTS

S 1. *Sentence skills:* ORAL READING: Read sentences with appropriate intonation.
- 1 — 4-7 Words
- 2 — 8-14 Words/Quotes
- 3 — 15-24 Words/Dramatic

S 2. *Sentence skills:* SPACES BETWEEN WORDS: Recognize and produce spaces between words.
- 1

S 3. *Sentence skills:* SENTENCE MEMORY: Reproduce sentences of increasing complexity.
- 1 — 3-5 Words
- 2 — 5-8 Words

S 4. *Sentence skills:* DICTATION: Write dictated sentences.
- 1, 2, 3, 4 — Frequencies 1-300
- 5 — 301-600
- 6 — 601-1000

GRAMMATICAL ASPECTS

S 5. *Sentence skills:* CAPITALIZATION: Use capitals correctly.
- 1 Initial Words Names
- 2 Place Names
- 3 Titles Initials
- 4 Time
- 5 Address Organization
- 6 Religious
- 7 Vehicles Plants Animals
- 8 Trade names
- 9 Quotes
- 10 Titles

S 6. *Sentence skills:* PUNCTUATION: Use punctuation marks correctly.
- 1 Marks
- 2 ⊙
- 3 ⑦
- 4 ①
- 5 ⊙
- 6 ⊙
- 7 Direct quotes
- 8 Compound sentence
- 9 Series
- 10 Interjections
- 11 Appositive
- 12 Antithetical
- 13 Dates Places
- 14 Parenthetical elements
- 15 Mistaken junctions
- 16 Intro-clauses
- 17 Nonrestrictive
- 18 Sentence break
- 19 Series
- 20 ⊙
- 21 Combination

S 7. *Sentence skills:* TRANSFORMATIONS: Rewrite sentences to fulfill grammatical constraints.
- 1 Singular
- 2 Plural
- 3 Negation
- 4 Pronoun
- 5 Pronoun
- 6 Tense: Present
- 7 Tense: Past
- 8 Tense: Future
- 9 Aux. have
- 10 Aux. be
- 11 Aux. be + have
- 12 Passive
- 13 Links
- 14 Links
- 15 Links
- 16 Links
- 17 Word order

REFERENTIAL ASPECTS

S 8. *Sentence skills:* DIRECTIONS: Follow workbook and test directions.
- 1 Circle Underline Cross out
- 2 Draw Make Put

S 9. *Sentence skills:* QUESTIONS: Produce questions controlled by answers.
- 1 Who
- 2 What
- 3 Where
- 4 When
- 5 Why
- 6 How

S 10. *Sentence skills:* SENTENCE MEANING: Choose meanings which conform to particular constraints.
- 1 Picture constraint
- 2 Internal constraint (sense)
- 3 External constraint (paragraph)

S 11. *Sentence skills:* FIGURATIVE LANGUAGE: Recognize idioms and similes.
- 1 Recognize idioms
- 2 Recognize idioms
- 3 Recognize idioms
- 4 Interpret similes

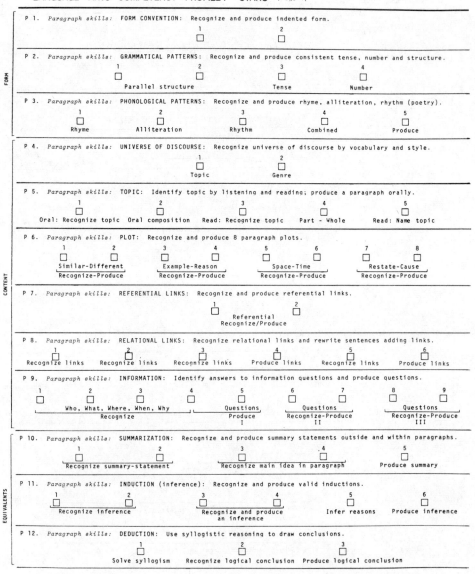

LANGUAGE ARTS COMPETENCY PROFILE: STARS (Page 4)

FORM

P 1. *Paragraph skills:* FORM CONVENTION: Recognize and produce indented form.
1   2

P 2. *Paragraph skills:* GRAMMATICAL PATTERNS: Recognize and produce consistent tense, number and structure.
1   2   3   4
Parallel structure   Tense   Number

P 3. *Paragraph skills:* PHONOLOGICAL PATTERNS: Recognize and produce rhyme, alliteration, rhythm (poetry).
1   2   3   4   5
Rhyme   Alliteration   Rhythm   Combined   Produce

CONTENT

P 4. *Paragraph skills:* UNIVERSE OF DISCOURSE: Recognize universe of discourse by vocabulary and style.
1   2
Topic   Genre

P 5. *Paragraph skills:* TOPIC: Identify topic by listening and reading; produce a paragraph orally.
1   2   3   4   5
Oral: Recognize topic   Oral composition   Read: Recognize topic   Part - Whole   Read: Name topic

P 6. *Paragraph skills:* PLOT: Recognize and produce 8 paragraph plots.
1   2   3   4   5   6   7   8
Similar-Different   Example-Reason   Space-Time   Restate-Cause
Recognize-Produce   Recognize-Produce   Recognize-Produce   Recognize-Produce

P 7. *Paragraph skills:* REFERENTIAL LINKS: Recognize and produce referential links.
1   2
Referential
Recognize/Produce

P 8. *Paragraph skills:* RELATIONAL LINKS: Recognize relational links and rewrite sentences adding links.
1   2   3   4   5   6
Recognize links   Recognize links   Recognize links   Produce links   Recognize links   Produce links

P 9. *Paragraph skills:* INFORMATION: Identify answers to information questions and produce questions.
1   2   3   4   5   6   7   8   9
Who, What, Where, When, Why   Questions   Questions   Questions
Recognize   Produce   Recognize-Produce   Recognize-Produce
I   II   III

EQUIVALENTS

P 10. *Paragraph skills:* SUMMARIZATION: Recognize and produce summary statements outside and within paragraphs.
1   2   3   4   5
Recognize summary-statement   Recognize main idea in paragraph   Produce summary

P 11. *Paragraph skills:* INDUCTION (inference): Recognize and produce valid inductions.
1   2   3   4   5   6
Recognize inference   Recognize and produce   Infer reasons   Produce inference
an inference

P 12. *Paragraph skills:* DEDUCTION: Use syllogistic reasoning to draw conclusions.
1   2   3
Solve syllogism   Recognize logical conclusion   Produce logical conclusion

LANGUAGE ARTS COMPETENCY PROFILE: STARS (Page 5)

P 13. *Paragraph skills:* FOCUS: Identify focus (setting, topic, action, time, motive).

1	2	3	4	5
☐	☐	☐	☐	☐
Select focus	Recognize time & motive	Recognize setting description	Recognize topic description	Recognize action description

P 14. *Paragraph skills:* POINT OF VIEW: Recognize and produce paragraph reflecting point of view.

1	2	3	4
☐	☐	☐	☐
Recognize point of view (who)	Produce paragraph from a point of view	Recognize pro or con point of view	Produce pro or con point of view

P 15. *Paragraph skills:* MOOD: Recognize mood.

1	2	3
☐	☐	☐
Sad Happy	Mysterious Adventurous	Humorous Serious

P 16. *Paragraph skills:* ORAL READING:(dramatic): Read aloud with appropriate intonation.

1	2	3	4
☐	☐	☐	☐
Essay & Drama	Essay & Drama	Story	Poetry

B 1. *Book skills:* FICTION: Recognize and produce fictional works.

1	2	3	4	5	6	7
☐	☐	☐	☐	☐	☐	☐
Reference data	Genre	Book report	Write stories: Character	Write stories: Setting	Write stories: Action	Write stories: Motivation

B 2. *Book skills:* NONFICTION: Recognize and produce nonfictional works.

1	2	3	4	5
☐	☐	☐	☐	☐
Reference data	Genre	Research	Organize report	Produce report

B 3. *Book skills:* TEXTBOOKS: Use a textbook properly.

1	2	3	4	5	6	7
☐	☐	☐	☐	☐	☐	☐
Orientation	Reference data		Skimming	Formulate study questions	Answer study questions	Technical terms

B 4. *Book skills:* REFERENCE WORKS: Use appropriate reference works.

1	2	3	4	5	6	7	8	9
☐	☐	☐	☐	☐	☐	☐	☐	☐
Dictionary		Encyclopedia			Thesaurus	Almanac	Library	

B 5. *Book skills:* PERIODICALS: Find and use books and newspapers.

1	2	3	4	5
☐	☐	☐	☐	☐
Newspaper	Newspapers	Magazines	Newspapers	

B 6. *Book skills:* LETTERS: Identify letter format; write letters for differing purposes.

1	2	3	4	5	6
☐	☐	☐	☐	☐	☐
Recognize format	Produce format	Recognize format	Produce format	Produce letter of complaint	Respond to a survey

IMPACT

The array of tests is presented by level, beginning with letter skills and ending with book skills. Within any level, tests are grouped (left margin) to conform with the interlocking matrix. Despite some nomenclature differences, the model and the reality are closely similar. But certain of the differences are notable. The model distinguishes letter **names** (Associative) and letter **sounds** (Structural). The author of the tests, Judith M. Smith, viewed names and sounds both as Associative (or Equivalents, to use her nomenclature), thus emphasizing the acquisition of paired associates rather than the **function** of letter-sound equivalents during reading.

At the word and sentence levels, the linguistic terms **grammatical** and **referential** are analogous to the terms **structural** and **functional** in the model. At the paragraph level, the terms **content** and **impact** seem to imply structure and function, while **form** and **equivalents** seem to imply perceptual and associative tasks.

At the level of discourse, the tests depart from the model to focus on typical school tasks, although some aspects of discourse are represented (e.g., literary forms = genre).

Since the model's primary function is to suggest tasks for measurement rather than to require them, the similarity between the model and the battery need not be complete. Therefore, straining to articulate them may be pedantic.

III. The Impact of Measurement on Achievement

In a sense, this book is aimed toward the definition and measurement of reading and writing competencies. Improvement in instruction has been slow over the past century; great emotion has been expended by proponents of various methods of instruction; instructional programs and systems have proliferated so that, at the present writing, there are more than 100 such products on the market. The whole miasmic picture has been ably documented by Chall (1967).

And the primary reason? There has been no substantial agreement on what should be measured, on a definition of what constitutes competency in reading and writing. The question has virtually always been, Which method is better? when it should have been, What is the goal and how can we reach it? If the goal were a given standard of literacy and if it were attained, then we might well ask which method is better, in terms of its being cheaper or faster and having fewer negative side effects.

Who knows what might happen if both teachers and children knew the goals of instruction? Figure 6.3 shows what happened under those conditions in one study. In 1972, criterion tests of cursive writing were administered to fourth-grade children over a 2-week period. In 1973, every fourth-grade child had

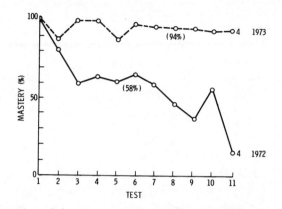

Figure 6.3. Proportion of fourth-grade children who achieved 100% scores on tests of cursive writing with use of criterion-referenced tests (1973) and without (1972).

available to him a booklet of the tests, gradated from easy to difficult. Children were allowed to take the tests as they were ready for them. "Mastery" in the figure refers to the proportion of fourth-graders in the total school system who achieved 100% on each of 11 tests. In 1972, those proportions were 98% (test 1), 80% (test 2), 60% (test 3), and so on. The following year, when teachers and children were in a position to target on the tests, achievement was substantially higher.

*   *   *   *   *

This chapter has presented a view of criterion-referenced tests as the product of an engineering effort designed to uncover a stimulus domain. For reading (and writing), the domain is presented as an interlocking hierarchy consisting of units (contours, letters, etc.) and levels of learning (perceptual, associative, structural, and functional). The analysis yields recognizable subskills for which criterion-referenced tests can be constructed. An outline of such a set of tests was presented.

A brief consideration of motivation will be presented in the next chapter.

MOTIVATION AS
ATTENTIONAL CONTROL

JIMMY'S STORY

I began teaching English in the high school of a university town. As newest teacher, I was assigned those students who were least likely to be damaged, the potential dropouts and the college-bound. During that first year, I discovered what most teachers discover: There was little that was relevant to the classroom in most of the teacher-training courses I had taken. In particular, I wondered what should be done about the Jimmys of the world: Jimmy O'Brien, tall, cool, a womanizer at age 15, IQ of 135. Jimmy was the laggard of the slow group.

After trying for two semesters to move Jimmy off dead-center, I re-enrolled in the university to find out what the psychologists had to say about motivating the Jimmys. I discovered that they had a good deal to say about many things, but motivation was not one of them, at least the motivation of schoolchildren (food deprivation? water deprivation? electric shock?).

I returned for a second year of teaching and discovered that Jimmy was still with me. Good! Another chance! And another failure. Never mind Otto, who went from the slow group to a distinguished career in the theater. Or Turk, IQ 82, who was accepted by the university and starred on the wrestling team for 2 years before they found him out. What worried me were the Jimmys, the ones who had everything and did nothing.

113

Seventeen years later, I found what I thought might be the answer. It happened like this:

All preparations had been made for the new crop of readers coming to the University of Michigan Reading Center for help. The programmed curriculum was complete; a teacher highly trained in classroom-management techniques was ready (no praise, no punishment, just rule enforcement); and the one-way windows had been installed. Motivation was not expected to be a problem because the children would be successful in the materials—and, as everyone knows, "Success is its own reward." (That little homily was the extent of my knowledge about motivation after 17 years.)

The children went to work with a will—that is, four of the six did. The other two were allowed to sit without doing anything. We assumed they would begin when they got sufficiently bored. And they did begin after a few days. But at the end of 2 weeks, the operation started to go sour. One boy began acting out. Three others seemed afraid to go to their desks. They had been successful. Could it be that they feared success? The class was continued.

The children began to wander, to look up the chimney from the fireplace, to press their faces against the one-way window in order to catch the observers ("I see one!"), to hover near the outside windows. One day they brought all their chairs together in the center of the room and huddled there. What was most upsetting was that they had everything we could offer and were doing nothing. (Their work curves appear in Figure 1.1.)

A staff conference was called to determine the missing ingredient. The only answer came from the assistant director, Skinner-trained, who said, "Obviously, they aren't getting reinforced." "But," I said, "what about success! Isn't that reinforcing?" "Apparently not. They aren't working." Skinner-trained psychologists say that kind of thing.

So, I capitulated: "OK. Use your M & M's or tokens or whatever. It disturbs me because we aren't going to be able to do it in the schools. But I give up."

Two new groups began at that time. One was put on an intermittent schedule of reinforcement using pennies; it was set up so the children would not be able to predict time of occurrence or amount of payoff. The other group was put on a continuous schedule of reinforcement, in which the amount and the occurrence of payoff were predictable.

Both groups produced achievement at an accelerating rate, far beyond what the staff had ever experienced. It looked as though money were the answer.

But one day a strange event occurred. Hyperactive Joey was receiving his payoff from the secretary. He looked at his nickel "A nickel! Aww . . . I got twenty-five cents yesterday! Hmmm. I guess I wasn't working today!"

I witnessed little Joe's insight. "Ahhh," I said, "Is it possible that it's not the money that reinforces; is it possible that it's the information? Feedback of information on progress? That might mean that success is reinforcing, but that success is not enough. We also have to know that we're moving toward a goal, making progress!'' Whereupon, another group was started. This one received no money, just information. Each child graphed his work output, the number of tasks completed correctly each day.

The rate of work was virtually identical to that of the group on a continuous schedule of reinforcement with money.

* * * * *

Having a goal and receiving information on progress toward it: That is what Jimmy needed. But come to think of it, he may well have had goals, and notches on his belt for a measure, the goals and measures that some school failures substitute for school success.

The term **motivation,** in its simplest sense, may be translated as "what we pay attention to." The purposeful use of motivation by teachers to produce achieving children may be called the **control of attention.** The teacher's task with regard to motivation is to arrange conditions so that children come under the control of (i.e., pay attention to) instructional arrays.

Certain conditions in the learner and in the environment related to attentional control have been alluded to in early chapters. Learner conditions include uncertainty arousal and reduction and reflexive responses to threat. Environmental conditions include rule enforcement, task characteristics, and methods of providing information feedback.

I. Learner Conditions

A. *Uncertainty Reduction*

Uncertainty arousal and reduction were discussed in Chapter 4 with regard to how learning occurs. **Uncertainty** was defined as "a state of discomfort that exists when an organism is faced with a stimulus to which it has no appropriate response." Any response followed by removal of the stimulus reduces uncertainty. For example, Carmine is stuck on a problem. The problem constitutes a stimulus to which she has no appropriate response. She raises her hand to attract the teacher's attention, secure in her prediction that the teacher will come to her rescue. Here comes the teacher. Uncertainty drops. When faced with a problem on which she is stuck, she will tend to raise her hand. Her hand-raising behavior is called **dependency behavior.**

But what if the teacher did not come to her? Then Carmine would look toward the teacher. The teacher consitutes a stimulus to which Carmine has a response, but she would not be able to respond if the teacher did not come. Uncertainty would not be reduced. It might in fact increase. If the teacher does not ever respond to the raised hand, Carmine's hand-raising response will extinguish. And **if the task is doable** (as it was in Carmine's case), when she turns back to it, she may be able to do it, if not today, perhaps tomorrow. The sequence of events just described may be termed **establishing independence**.

According to the uncertainty principle, whatever behavior occurs immediately prior to uncertainty reduction will tend to occur on later, similar occasions. If school tasks are devised properly and if the environment is secure, most of the uncertainty can be encapsulated or controlled by the task, even for very anxious children.

B. Response to Threat

The peripheral retina is sensitive to movement. When such movement is apprehended, attention switches reflexly so that the moving stimulus is focused upon. Loud noises result in an alerting response, a readiness to perceive any threat. The more tense the organism (the higher the initial level of uncertainty), the less stimulation is required to alert him and to cause attentional shifts **(distractions)**. Instructional tasks, no matter how cleverly devised, cannot compete with such distractions without environmental support.

To the young child, the classroom is a jungle. He is surrounded by other young animals, largely unpredictable in their behavior. Furthermore, there is a powerful big animal, called *teacher,* who is also largely unpredictable. Most children remain constantly alert to the potential dangers around them. When they tire, they tend to erupt, to strike out, or, at the very least, to test the degree of predictability of those around them. Control of learner attention in a noisy, crowded, unpredictable environment is extremely difficult.

II. Environmental Conditions

One way to reduce uncertainty is to make an appropriate response when faced with a stimulus. A second way to reduce it is to predict the occurrence of an event and to have it occur. If the sequence of events could be verbalized, it might sound like this: "Yesterday, I raised my hand and the teacher came; if I raise my hand, the teacher will come. Ahhh, she's coming." Or, "Yesterday, my pencil fell on the floor and the teacher picked it up; here she comes—oops—she picked it up."

A. Rule Testing

The child's tendency to test the regularities or **rules** of the environment may be used by a teacher to satisfy the child's need for security—to reduce his tension and increase his concentration (the attentional control exerted by the task).

The teacher who is alert to rule-testing behavior will observe such behaviors occurring almost continuously—unless children are deeply engrossed in their work.

Although any regularity may be used for rule testing, the more predictable the sequence, the more likely it is to be tested. Whenever a child's uncertainty rises, and it is not encapsulated by tasks, he tests a rule and predicts that it will be enforced. If it is enforced, he relaxes and, often, returns to work.

How often must a rule be enforced to carry out its function of relaxing a child? There is little evidence available on this question. In one unpublished study of first-grade children, we counted the number of rule tests occurring in a 15-minute independent work period each day for 9 weeks. In addition, we counted the number of times the teacher enforced the rule ("No talking during independent work time." Enforcement: "Joe, the rule.") During the first 3 weeks, the teacher enforced the rule about half the time it was tested. Rule tests fluctuated from 30 to 40 in a 15-minute period over that time. During the fourth week, her enforcement rate rose to 80% and was maintained at that level. There was an immediate drop in rule tests to 5 in 15 minutes and a gradual decrease to a steady 2 tests per period for the entire group.

Based only on this data, we would recommend that a rule be enforced at least four out of five times that it is tested. But note that only one rule was used and this superior teacher enforced it only half the time. (Her rate rose to 80% only after she was given feedback on her rate of enforcement. And before the feedback, she had been quite sure she was enforcing 100% of the time.) Imagine the difficulty one would have in enforcing two or three or four rules—and most teachers have more rules than that.

Consistent, unemotional enforcement of one or two rules increases the predictability of behavior of the group and results in a relatively comfortable environment. The power of rule enforcement as a facilitator of attentional control is increased by having doable tasks.

B. Task Characteristics

Construction of tasks that will control attention has been discussed at length in Chapter 3. What should be pointed out here, however, is that children find well-designed tasks fun to do; such tasks exert a powerful control. Consider games that teach: hidden figures, crossword puzzles, dot-to-dot, and many others. An adequately programmed task will control the attention of the learner. It should be fun and interesting; the learner should enjoy doing it. A dull task is not adequately programmed.

On the other hand, it may not look interesting to an adult. Dot-to-dot books bore me—but, at certain ages, they did not bore my children. One might well suspend judgment until the material is tried out with children.

C. Information Feedback

The potential of information feedback as a pedagogical tool is difficult to assess. From present evidence [a series of doctoral studies[1] and a contribution by Powers (1973)], its power to control behavior appears to be formidable. The example given in Jimmy's Story earlier in this chapter seems to equate information with such a universal reinforcer as money.

The effectiveness of feedback as a tool for controlling attention is not limited to children. Feedback to the teacher on her rule-enforcement behavior brought an immediate improvement. Chapman (1973) and Markel (1974) have shown that the success of innovative projects is greatly facilitated by establishing feedback loops to a variety of decision makers and by timing the flow of information.

Methods of implementing feedback of information in the classroom have been described extensively elsewhere (D. E. P. Smith & J. M. Smith, 1975a, pp. 42–61).

The classroom is a system consisting of a teacher, children, tasks, measures, feedback signals, and interactions among these parts. It is a living, breathing organism and changes over time. Most of this book has focused attention on one part, instructional tasks, with lesser attention paid to measures and feedback.

Educational problems can be reduced in severity by improving instructional materials, but not eliminated. The continued existence of such problems is virtually always maintained by the larger social context. But we should not wait for the culture to optimize before improving classroom ecology: It may well be that such improvements will force the larger system toward health. First of all, to paraphrase Voltaire, we must tend our own gardens.

III. Behavior Modification as Self-Shaping

The term **behavior modification** refers to a set of techniques designed to increase the incidence of desirable behaviors and to decrease the incidence of

---

[1] D. M. Brethower, 1970; K. S. Brethower, 1973; R. E. Olds, 1970; R. E. Chapman, 1973; G. Markel, 1974; A. Gomon, 1974.

undesirable behaviors through the artful use of reinforcing and punishing consequences. Although the techniques have varied origins, their systematic and widespread use is commonly attributed to the influence of B. F. Skinner's writings. Applications are by now so widespread and successes are so pronounced that behavior modification may properly be described as a **movement** (McConnell, 1970). And movements generate controversy.

Attacks on behavior modifiers commonly focus on an inferred unwilling cooperation of the subject (Trotter & Warren, 1974). The trainer or teacher shapes the learner into conforming behavior or achievement by rewarding small changes in behavior in the direction of the norm or goal. Rewards commonly consist of candy, tokens (money), smiles, or praise.

It seems to me that the strategies possess two clear dangers, which have not been adequately explored: Who shall decide what is desirable behavior? What price do we pay when we reduce undesirable behaviors? The child's vulnerability, for example, his childish response to adult approval, is used as a tool to bring him around ("for his own good," of course). The inevitable question, then, concerns **who** shall decide what is good for the child. Skinner's answer that "men of good will" should decide is not very satisfactory (Skinner, 1961). I, for one, am unwilling to put myself into the hands of "men of good will." Such a belief as yesterday's "A woman's place is in the home," was undoubtedly held by "men of good will." "Have faith in your country's leaders!" speaks for itself.

The second danger results from our cultural view of "negative" behaviors. Aggressive behaviors, for example, tend to be deplored, not only by behavior modifiers but by virtually everyone. Therefore, such behaviors appear to be appropriate targets for the use of operant techniques. If a child attacks his peers, or cries easily, or destroys property, or breaks rules, such behaviors should be reduced or eliminated by training.

But just a moment! From a system point of view, if a negative behavior occurs it may serve a necessary function in the child's development. Thus, a negative behavior may remain at strength because it is being maintained by the behaviors of parents or teachers. If so, it will extinguish if ignored. But if it is functional in the learning economy of the child, it will not extinguish when ignored, and attempts to eliminate it may cause a new set of problems.

Temper tantrums serve as one example of aggressive behaviors that have a useful function (Smith & Smith, 1975d). Another example is rule testing. In a stable, safe classroom, rule testing occurs at a rate approximating one test or infraction per child-hour under ideal enforcement conditions. Although all normal children test rules, on a given day only a few may do so and those at a variable rate, depending on degree of emotionality. Rule testing may be viewed as an operant used by the child to allow him to focus on a task. If that is the case, we extinguish rule-testing behavior at our peril.

Whether or not the reader agrees that these examples justify tolerance for aggressive behaviors, they should give him pause. At least we should ask, Is there any way we can capitalize on the positives of behavior-modification techniques and still minimize our risks?

An alternative view of behavior modification is possible. Current strategies use the experimenter as decision maker: He knows the goal (the target stimulus) and shapes the learner toward it. But the learner himself can be put in the position of decision maker, of self-shaper.

Self-shaping is to be distinguished from experimenter shaping. In both cases, some final performance is produced by making renforcing stimuli contingent upon responses that approximate that performance. In the case of experimenter shaping, the standards for an adequate performance are known to the experimenter, who shapes the behavior of the learner. When the person doing the learning shapes himself, he must first learn the standards for evaluating the performance. In brief, he must learn what a good performance looks like and what is wrong with a bad performance. Such discriminations are precisely those necessary for teaching a target stimulus. The learner masters the target stimulus (and the appropriate standards) by observing adequate and inadequate models. He is then in a position to monitor his own behavior, rewarding himself for approximations to the goal and punishing himself for errors. He will apply reinforcers and punishers on the basis of the similarity between an actual behavior and an intended behavior.

A self-shaping system requires that the learner choose to participate in the learning activity. If he does not so choose, the teacher does not attempt to shape him into it by using non-task-related reinforcers such as candy or smiles. Rather, he reevaluates the proffered tasks to determine whether they are appropriate to this learner and/or whether the environment is conducive to performance of such tasks. For example, a ghetto child placed in a middle-class first grade has more important tasks to engage him than those used to learn reading. He must first learn a new complex of social skills and, perhaps, a new language. A frightened child may be unable to choose any task until he has brought his peers under control. Their presence may produce uncertainty far beyond that arising from the task.

What I am arguing is that, given a rich environment, information feedback, and a variety of options, the child will respond to tasks that are most appropriate for him at that time. The teacher's responsibility is to arrange environments for learning, with the end result that children will be in a position to construct their own environments. This is precisely the message of Skinner's volume, *Beyond Freedom and Dignity* (1972). He would have us surround ourselves with those stimuli that will elicit the responses we want to make—in essence, construct our own ideal environment.

INFORMATION FEEDBACK
IN EDUCATIONAL SYSTEMS

Awareness of consequences of a behavior may prove to be the most powerful motivating technique developed in modern-day education. Such awareness may be engineered by providing feedback loops in educational systems (Gomon, 1974; Markel, 1974).

To demonstrate the power of information feedback, I shall first define the terms **feedback** and **system**, then report a series of field studies illustrating ways educational systems have been modified by feedback intervention.[1]

[1] The studies reported herein constitute programmatic research conducted as doctoral studies by the staff and associates of the University of Michigan, Bureau of Psychological Services, Reading and Study Skills Center, from 1969 to 1975.

Topic	Reference
Engineering: students	D. E. P. Smith, Brethower, & Cabot (1969)
Latency	Olds (1970)
Definition: adaptive systems	D. M. Brethower (1970)
Engineering: teachers	Heiman (1970)
Positive versus negative feedback	Walter (1971)
Engineering: industrial	K. S. Brethower (1973)
Taxonomy: classroom measures	Chapman (1973)
Engineering: classroom innovation	G. Markel (1974)
Innovative process	Gomon (1974)

I. Feedback Defined

As defined by D. M. Brethower (1970), feedback is "information about system performance used to modify system performance." Olds (1970) carried the definition further:

> Feedback is performance information which is (*1*) external [observable], (*2*) displayed in some way over time, (*3*) related to some parameter of the response, and (*4*) response modifying or response maintaining over time. . . . In order for performance information to qualify as feedback, it must be demonstrated that the information has exerted **control** over the performance. This is a restrictive notion in that not all performance information **fed back** to the performer qualifies as feedback [pp. 5–8].

For example, in classroom studies, Chapman reported that one measure, **teacher observation of student task-related data,** was unrelated to success of an innovative practice; another measure, **teacher observation of student goal-related data,** was highly related to success (1973). The first measure would not qualify as information feedback; the second measure would so qualify.

Characteristics of signals that work as feedback have been suggested by K. Brethower (1973). In a series of studies of feedback systems in a petrochemical company and an air freight company, she identified two characteristics as critical:

(*1*) The measured performance to be used as feedback must be valued by the organization (**value**).

(*2*) Employees are able to see that the measures are clearly related to their job performance (**relevance**).

These characteristics are reiterated in Chapman's measures of school variables, to be reported later in this chapter.

A further distinction has been clarified by Walter (1971): **on-target** and **off-target** information. When teachers fed back information on achievement gain (on target) to a group of unruly children, achievement increased and unruly behavior decreased. When information on unruly behavior (rule testing: off target) was fed back, unruly behavior decreased but so did achievement gains. Stuart has discussed this phenomenon (1974, pp. 24ff.) and concluded that "it seems invariably wise to begin with the acceleration of a desired response . . . and only later resort to decelerative techniques to do away with any problem behavior that persists [p. 24]."

To recapitulate, a feedback signal controls the behavior of the receiver; it must seem relevant to him and valuable to his superior.

II. System Defined

Dale Brethower has done a great deal to clarify the concept of a learning system, particularly a self-shaping, self-modifying, **adaptive** system. The following section is excerpted from materials he has prepared for student use:[2]

a. What is an Educational System?

One way of describing an educational system is to draw a picture of it. The following picture has proven useful.

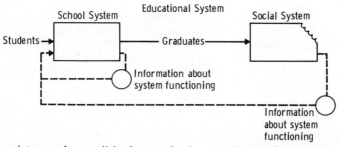

The picture makes explicit that a school system is related to the larger social system; however, it does not attempt to show what the relationship is. For example, an educational system, e.g. a trade school, might attempt to train people for specific jobs whereas another educational system, e.g. a liberal arts college, might attempt to avoid job training, concentrating on nonvocational aims.

The picture calls attention to two types of information essential to the proper functioning of a school system. One type of information comes from the school system itself, e.g. the number and kinds of students who matriculate and graduate, the cost of operating, the numbers and kinds of courses taught. The other type of information comes from the social system, e.g. the fate of graduates, the curriculum needs, the degree of support for education. (The notched corner of the Social System rectangle symbolizes relatively incomplete knowledge about the social system.)

The picture calls attention to the main activity of school systems: transformation of "students" into "graduates." Other activities such as scholarship and research could be emphasized by relabeling the diagram or by adding other arrows to it.

b. What Are the Parts of an Educational System?

An educational system, according to the point of view being put forth here, has the six parts shown on the diagram:

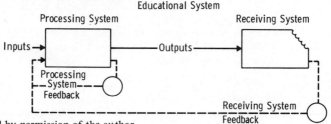

[2] Reprinted by permission of the author.

Thus any educational system has some kind and quantity of inputs and a processing system for transforming these inputs into an output. For example, the input to a community college would be students from the area. The registration, counseling and teaching procedures would make up the processing system. Processing system feedback would be concerned with such items as percentages of students passing certain courses, graduating, etc. The Receiving System might be local businesses and nearby colleges and universities. Receiving System feedback would be concerned with the success of graduates, their involvement in community affairs, etc.

The notched corner of the Receiving System rectangle symbolizes incomplete information about the Receiving System. It also symbolizes that the Receiving System, while a crucial part of the educational system, is a part of it in a rather unique sense. It is a part in a transactional or interactive sense rather than in an authoritarian sense. Using the community college as an example, the administration and governing faculty can exert rather authoritarian control over the Processing System but not over the Receiving System. To use an analogy, the Processing System and the Receiving System are symbiotic in their relationship—each needs the other.

c. How Do the Parts of an Educational System Interact?

The interaction of the parts of educational systems revolves around the concepts of goals, objectives and feedback.

Goals: According to our usage, goals specify the desired interaction between the Processing System and the Receiving System.
Objectives: Objectives specify the desired outputs of a Processing System.
Feedback: Feedback is information used to guide performance toward goals and objectives.

An example will help to illustrate the intent of the statements above. Consider a remedial reading service operating within a public school:

A Remedial Reading System

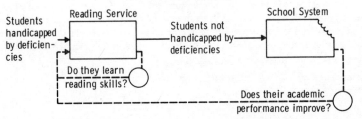

The **Goals** of the Reading Service would relate to the goals of the school. Without specifying school goals in detail, we can state the goals for the Reading Service: Improve academic achievement by reducing reading related handicaps. (And, to do so with a given budget of time, funds, materials, etc.) The **Receiving System Feedback** would, therefore, be information regarding improvement in academic achievement of students served. The **Objectives** for the Reading Service would then be set in terms of the number of students to be served and the particular reading skills to improve. The **Processing System Feedback** would be information regarding improvement in the reading skills.

Brethower goes on to demonstrate a system view as applied to the lowest subsystem, the individual learner, and to the total school system. For the individual, internal feedback consists of an answer to the question, How am I doing? whereas external feedback consists of an answer to the question, How do others think I'm doing?

III. Engineering a School Innovation

Three extensive studies demonstrate both surprising and impressive results of the feedback model and a model of research procedures. The studies are those of Chapman (1973), Markel (1974), and Gomon (1974).

(*1*) First, Chapman investigated the measurable variables operating in the classrooms, in an attempt to ascertain which are related to increased student achievement. He gathered data on 31 variables in 12 innovative projects during one school year. By objective means, he determined that 4 projects were clearly successful and 4 were clearly unsuccessful. He then found that 5 of the 31 measures differentiated successful from unsuccessful projects.

(2) Markel followed by monitoring 6 new, innovative projects for a year. She established measures of the 5 variables identified by Chapman, developed feedback loops to the various receivers (children, teacher, principal, and community) and did what was necessary to keep all loops operating. She thereby produced 6 successful projects.

(*3*) Gomon applied this knowledge of how to sustain an innovation by operating a language-learning laboratory within a school system. She then observed and documented resulting reactive changes in the larger system.

A. *The Chapman Study*

As an evaluator in a large, Midwest school system, Chapman was aware of the current concept of evaluation as feedback for decision making (Guba & Stufflebeam, 1970; Scriven, 1967). But feedback of what? One must isolate all relevant variables and determine which ones are indicators of program success, i.e., feedback variables in the sense defined herein. He was concerned both with the training system and with the receiving system. With regard to the latter, he stated that "accountability may be defined, in relation to feedback, as that event in a Receiving System (such as a school district) in which the feedback presented is compared with promised results (such as student performance data) followed by appropriate consequences to the staff of the Training System (such as contractors or teachers) [Chapman, 1973, p. 12]."

He searched the literature in order to identify relevant variables, developed measures of them, then compared their occurrence in successful and unsuccessful projects. These independent variables appear in Figure 8.1 (articulated with the Brethower model).

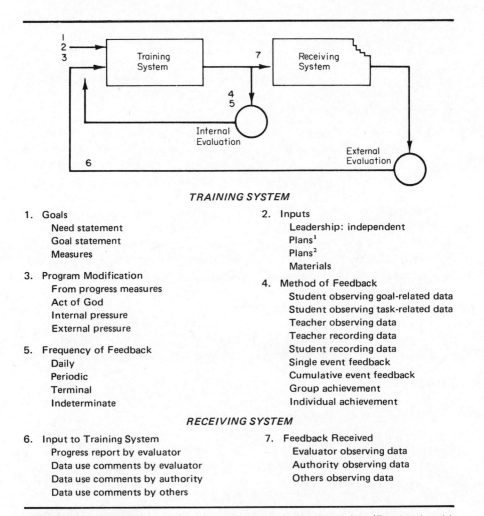

TRAINING SYSTEM

1. Goals
   Need statement
   Goal statement
   Measures

3. Program Modification
   From progress measures
   Act of God
   Internal pressure
   External pressure

5. Frequency of Feedback
   Daily
   Periodic
   Terminal
   Indeterminate

2. Inputs
   Leadership: independent
   Plans[1]
   Plans[2]
   Materials

4. Method of Feedback
   Student observing goal-related data
   Student observing task-related data
   Teacher observing data
   Teacher recording data
   Student recording data
   Single event feedback
   Cumulative event feedback
   Group achievement
   Individual achievement

RECEIVING SYSTEM

6. Input to Training System
   Progress report by evaluator
   Data use comments by evaluator
   Data use comments by authority
   Data use comments by others

7. Feedback Received
   Evaluator observing data
   Authority observing data
   Others observing data

Figure 8.1. Independent variables related to the feedback model. (Reprinted, with permission, from *Evaluation as feedback in innovative school programs,* by R. E. Chapman, 1973.)

Variables that distinguished successful from unsuccessful projects were these:

TRAINING SYSTEM

Goals   Method of Feedback
- Goal statement (written)   Student observing goal-related data
- Measures (of goals)   Student reecording (own) data

RECEIVING SYSTEM

Feedback Received
- Authority observing data

Chapman's results are consistent with those reported by Karen Brethower (value and relevance) found in an industrial setting. It should be noted that Chapman found sufficient evidence for the discriminative power of certain other variables to recommend their further study:

TRAINING SYSTEM

Feedback Method

Teacher observes goal data
Teacher records goal data
Single event feedback
Cumulative event feedback
Group achievement
Individual goal achievement

Feedback Frequency

Daily goal

RECEIVING SYSTEM

Input to Training System

Data use comments by authority (reinforcing remarks)

Feedback Received

Evaluator observes goal data
Others observe data

B. The Markel Study

Geraldine Markel worked in the Office of Research and Evaluation, Ann Arbor (Michigan) Public Schools (as did Chapman), under the direction of Dr. Patricia Carrigan. Dr. Markel served as an evaluation consultant to teachers and groups of teachers planning innovative projects. Her functions included training teachers in task analysis, writing objectives, developing measures, charting, facilitating procurement of instructional resources, liason with authorities, and dissemination of results.

Following Chapman's lead, she defined four feedback loops (Figure 8.2), made certain that teachers developed measures to be used as signals in each loop and, by means of modeling, by reinforcing successive approximations, by charm, and by other behavior modifying techniques, she saw that signals were sent to appropriate decision makers at appropriate times.

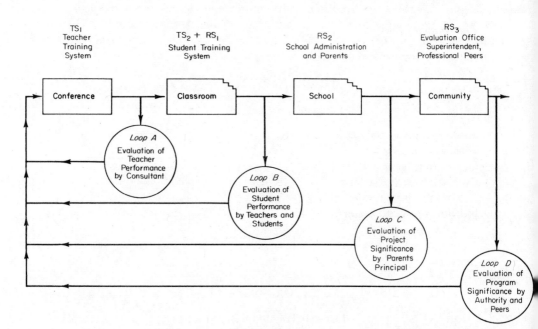

Figure 8.2. An educational training and receiving system with four feedback loops. Four systems are depicted, each with at least one feedback loop. The first, teacher training system 1 (TS_1) is controlled by the consultant who collects performance data on all teachers allowing for modification of the system. The first receiving system (RS_1), the classrooms, are controlled by the teachers who collect student performance data and modify instructional events. This receiving system is the student training system (TS_2) and student performances from it are received in a second receiving system (RS_2). This second receiving system is comprised of the principal and parents. Information for RS_2 influences both training systems, as well as itself. Lastly, information on performance is received by a third receiving system. This receiving system is composed of the consultant's supervisor and professional peers, and influences the teacher training system (TS_1). (Reprinted, with permission, from *The evaluation consultant and innovative elementary projects in an educational system*, by G. Markel, 1974.)

To simplify the monitoring task, she developed the chart shown in Figure 8.3. The progress of an innovative project is displayed in Figure 8.4.

Perhaps the most remarkable point here, aside from the demonstrated lawfulness of the engineering effort, was the success of **every** project (defined as successful completion of all steps in the evaluation process and the attainment of major project objectives). Not surprisingly to those who study educational innovations, the Office of Research and Evaluation, including the positions of consultant, evaluator, and director, were eliminated from the school budget. This "immolative" act appears less irrational after one reviews Gomon's study of the innovative process (1974).

C. The Gomon Study

When an instructional unit within an educational system operates effectively and efficiently, how does the system respond to it? Do changes occur in the system? In the subsystem? If so, what are the dynamics of change? When innovators charge the schools with being resistant to change, are they justified? Or is the change process itself lawful, so that innovators' criticisms reflect failures in engineering rather than encrusted monolithic institutions?

Audrey Gomon provides a number of answers to these questions in her report of *Systems Communication Patterns: An Institution's Response to an Innovation* (1974). The innovation was a "self-contained classroom instructional system, a language-learning laboratory, which (*1*) demonstrated accountable student achievement outcomes, (*2*) models effective learning conditions, (*3*) was developed in an institutionsl problem-solver perspective, and (*4*) functions under applied research constraints, modifying its operation in response to student performance information [abstract, p. 1]."

In more concrete terms:

> During 1970–1971 a language learning laboratory in a suburban midwestern high school of 2200 students provided instruction in basic and advanced language competencies for 817 sophomores with threse results:
>
> 1. 96% of the students met minimum requirements for 1/2 credit in English.
> 2. 80% chose and achieved the five competencies considered essential by the lab teachers.
>
> In the first semester only:
>
> 3. 417 students produced 5133 achievement units (M = 12.0). Cost: $5.50/unit.
>
> In the second semester only:
>
> 4. 400 students produced 7030 achievement units (M = 18.0). Cost: $3.60/unit.
> 5. 16% of the students achieved a second 1/2 English credit in one semester's time.
>
> In addition, English grade point averages increased significantly for students after the lab experience, and 75 students, who would have been grouped for remedial instruction previously, performed in regular classes with no increase in the proportion of failures in those classes.

= Proposed Deadline
+ = Positive Answer
− = Negative Answer
± = Incomplete Answer
GO = Proceed to Next Step
NO = Stop

8 EVALUATION STEPS

4 FEEDBACK LOOPS

					9/1/71	9/15/71	9/30/71	10/15/71	11/15/71	12/15/71	1/30/72	2/20/72	3/15/72	4/15/72	5/15/72	5/30/72	6/15/72	6/30/72	7/15/72	6/30/73
Loop D — Central Administration and University Use Student Performance (Out of School)	Loop C — Principal and Parents Use Student Performance (In School)	Loop B — Teacher Uses Student Performance (In Class)	Loop A — Consultant Uses Teacher Performance (In Meetings)	**Review original proposal**																
				Objectives																
				Measures																
				Feedback																
				Instruction																
				1. ASSESSMENT																
				Current year?																
				2. OBJECTIVES																
				Written statement?																
				Criterion Stated?																
				3. FEEDBACK																
				Measures Suitable?																
				Forms Designed?																
				Forms Ready to Use?																
				4. INSTRUCTION																
				Academic Materials?																
				Management Procedures?																
				5. MODIFICATION																
				Data Collected?																
				Data Visible?																
				Data Used by Teacher?																
				Data Used by Students?																
				6. EVALUATION																
				Assessments Made?																
				Analysis Done?																
				Report Outline?																
				Teacher Satisfied?																
				Final Report Written?																
				Data to Principal?																
				Feedback from Principal?																
				Data to Parents?																
				Questionnaire to Parents?																
				Feedback from Parents?																
				Project Continued?																
				7. DISSEMINATION																
				To Other Schools?																
				To Evaluation Office?																
				To Superintendent?																
				To University Conferences?																
				Gain Others' Models?																
				Used Others' Models?																
				8. REEVALUATION																
				Project Continued?																
				Data Collected & Used?																

Figure 8.3. A model feedback form for individual projects. (Reprinted, with permission, from *The evaluation consultant and innovative elementary projects in an educational system,* by G. Markel, 1974.)

KEY:

```
                                        · = Proposed Deadline
                                        + = Positive Answer
8 EVALUATION STEPS                      - = Negative Answer
4 FEEDBACK LOOPS                        ± = Incomplete Answer
                                        GO = Proceed to Next Step
                                        NO = Stop
```

Loop D = Central Administration and University Use Student Performance (Out of School)
Loop C = Principal and Parents Use Student Performance (In School)
Loop B = Teacher Uses Student Performance (In Class)
Loop A = Consultant Uses Teacher Performance (In Meetings)

	9/1/71	9/15/71	9/30/71	10/15/71	11/15/71	12/15/71	1/30/72	2/20/72	3/15/72	4/15/72	5/15/72	5/30/72	6/15/72	6/30/72	7/15/72	6/30/73
Review original proposal																
Objectives	±															
Measures	+															
Feedback	+															
Instruction	+															
1. ASSESSMENT																
Current year?				-	+											
2. OBJECTIVES					GO											
Written statement?				-	+											
Criterion Stated?				-	+											
3. FEEDBACK					GO											
Measures Suitable?				-	+											
Forms Designed?				+	+											
Forms Ready to Use?				-	+											
4. INSTRUCTION							GO									
Academic Materials?				+			+									
Management Procedures?				+			+									
5. MODIFICATION							GO			GO						
Data Collected?				.	+		+			+						
Data Visible?					+		+			+						
Data Used by Teacher?					+		+			+						
Data Used by Students?					-		+			+						
6. EVALUATION										GO						
Assessments Made?										+						
Analysis Done?											+					
Report Outline?											+					
Teacher Satisfied?											+					
Final Report Written?											-		+			
Data to Principal?							±		±							
Feedback from Principal?							±		+		GO					
Data to Parents?							-				±					
Questionnaire to Parents?							-				±					
Feedback from Parents?							+					+				
Project Continued?												+				
7. DISSEMINATION										GO		GO				
To Other Schools?												+				
To Evaluation Office?				+								+				
To Superintendent?				+								+				
To University Conferences?				+								+				
Gain Others' Models?							+					+				
Used Others' Models?							-					+				
8. REEVALUATION																GO
Project Continued?																+
Data Collected & Used?																+

Figure 8.4. Feedback form for Project III: art class. (Reprinted, with permission, from *The evaluation consultant and innovative elementary projects in an educational system,* by G. Markel, 1974.)

131

Operating characteristics of the language learning laboratory were these:

1. Opportunity for self-selection of learning objectives and self-pacing by students.
2. Use of independent learning tasks with teacher-ensured effectiveness.
3. Use of criterion-referenced assessment of achievement.
4. Availability of feedback on achievement and progress to a goal for students and teachers.
5. Ongoing modification of environmental contingencies to permit and support productive behavior by all students.
6. Use of group results for program modifications [Gomon, 1974, pp. 1–3].

In brief, this was an "adaptive performance system." During the first 4 years of its operation, it had an impact on the school and school system, and it was itself changed. Systems communications (all recorded events that might be viewed as output or feedback signals) were analyzed by identifying them "as to their origin (teachers, administrators outsiders), the consequence message they carry (facilitation [of the efforts of the lab], immolation [attacks], imitation [of the lab and its operation]), and the reality level of change they effect or reject (commitment [lip service], structural context [actual change in classload, etc.], classroom activity) [abstract, p. 2]."

The method of study is illustrated by a table taken from the report. (See Table 8.1.) All events were recorded and coded. The incidence of the various kinds of response (for example, immolative or imitative) was graphed over eight semesters.

Patterns of negative (immolative) and positive (facilitative and/or imitative) responses over eight semesters are shown in Figure 8.5. The extinction of negative responses over time and the eventual dominance of positive responses is clear. These patterns can be seen more dramatically in Figure 8.6.

The similarity between these curves and the learning and extinction curves of individual learners is striking and probably not adventitious. Analysis of events occurring at high points supports an interpretation of a sequence of learning activities by the school faculty as reflected in Figure 8.7.

In brief, evidences of conflict are followed by crises, faculty confrontation. At each occurrence (semesters 3 and 7), the lab staff responded to the crisis by presenting the "models" of new practices in contrast with the "foils" of old practices. "The pros and cons fought it out, thereby clarifying the similarities and distinctions of the old and the new. The argument was noisy, requiring the attention of all. As the distinctions gained precision through their juxtaposition, the policy decisions matched the innovative component to the more abstract goals of the school. . . . Now I see what it really is! [Gomon, 1974, p. 146]."

Each crisis is then followed by a "resolution" during which imitative activities spurt.

The stages of the system's response to the innovation are described by Gomon as follows:

A Proposed Model of the Innovative Process

Stage I: Intrusion

or

Does This Mean I'll Have to Change. . .

When an innovation, demonstrating efficiency in meeting an objective of the institution, intrudes a social structure, conflict will occur between the denigrative responses of those who share role characteristics with the innovators, and the integrative responses of those farthest from the potential requirements for personal change.

Stage II: Synergetic Crisis

or

Let's Make a Policy . . .

When the conflict engendered by innovative intrusion intensifies, the synergetic effect is to set the conditions for learning the innovation by (*1*) demanding the attention of the institution, (*2*) forcing a crisis through the requirement to make a policy level decision and (*3*) focusing the distinctions required to learn the innovation.

Stage III: Discrimination

or

Now I See . . .

When the first conflict–crisis response to an innovation's intrusion is resolved in the decision-making process, first level learnings of the innovation are demonstrated in policies reflecting the innovative components. When further instruction is provided, a high incidence of replications of the innovation occurs among those needing only enabling skills.

Stage IV: Exegetic Crisis

or

Let's Go Home Again . . .

When the innovation appears to be spreading through learning, crippling attacks on the model effect a second crisis—the crisis of critical analysis—when a return to tradition is effected by the required withdrawal of the innovators and by implications of the innovation's instability which preclude further imitation.

Stage V: Indigenous Expression

or

This Was My Idea . . .

When the unsatisfactory attempt to return to tradition forces the reality of changedness into focus, institutional personnel achieve an awareness of their new self and demonstrate this in their independent productions and gradual mutations of the innovation—since it is their own now.

The model of the innovative process is sensible in terms of the present report; further applications are needed to determine its universality. The simplicity and utility of the model is evidenced in the new principal's request of the learning specialist to get it all started again so that some functional staff development may occur in the school [Gomon, 1974, pp. 147–149].

Table 8.1
Sample Table from the Gomon Study[a]

Identification		Item Description	Classification								
Item	Month	Institutional Responses to Innovation	A	T	0	+	−	=	■	▲	●
1	Feb	Principal approves proposed course revision	A			+			■		
2	Mar	Assistant principal arranges time, space, p/t ratios	A			+				▲	
3	Mar	English department supports change proposal		T		+			■		
4	May	District approves production workshop			0	+					●
5	Aug	District Language Arts workshop uses products (#4) as source and model			0			=	■		
		Semester 1 Totals:	2 − 1 − 2 − 4 − 0 − 1 − 3 − 1 − 1								
6	Sep	Principal permits special grading system	A			+				▲	
7	Oct	Regional director denies special grading system			0		−			▲	
8	Oct	Regional director reconsiders, permits special grading system			0	+				▲	
9	Oct	Visiting parents support lab objectives			0	+			■		
10	Nov	English department censures grading, expresses lack of confidence in lab		T				x	■		
11	Jan	No English staff requests for diagnostic information: only 4 visit lab		T			−		■		
		Semester 2 Totals:	1 − 2 − 3 − 3 − 3 − 0 − 3 − 3 − 0								
12	Feb	Visitors note student independence, self-direction: request materials and operational guides			0	+					●
13	Feb	Faculty council questions permit for lab operation without their approval		T			−		■		
14	Mar	Faculty responses, re learning skills needed by students, are inarticulate and unanalyzable		T			−				●
15	May	Board of Education approves English elective changes with lab component			0	+			■		
16	May	Previously antagonistic English teacher volunteers to join lab staff		T		+					●
17	May	Central administration denies workshop for lab instructional material revision			0						●
18	Jun	Assistant principal directs final "I" recorded as "E" on student transcripts	A				−			▲	
19	Jun	Central administration approves lab staff product workshop for English literature material			0	+			■		
20	Jun	Administration ends flexible scheduling due to lack of central administration support	A				−			▲	
96	Jan	2 other district's high schools purchase lab material and staff training			0			=			●
97	Jan	Alternative school proposal uses lab components for operational design		T				=	■		
98	Jan	Another high school in the district uses Social Studies (#58 and 89) model to design psychology courses			0			=			●
99	Jan	Jr. high personnel refuse to screen accelerated students without seeing CRT's and course objectives for high school course			0			=			●
100	Jan	Students report innovative components as most effective learning conditions		T				=			●
101	Jan	Social Studies teacher (#89) constructs 3 mini courses following innovation model		T				=			●
102	Jan	3 Social Studies teachers request models and content aids from innovator (#101)		T				=	■		
		Semester 8 Totals:	1 − 13 − 7 − 3 − 1 − 7 − 8 − 0 − 13								
		4 Year Totals:	23 − 45 − 34 − 32 − 28 − 42 − 43 − 17 − 42								

[a]Reprinted, with permission, from *Systems communication patterns: An institution's response to an innovation*, by A. Gomon, 1974.

Table 8.1 *continued*

The signals and responses of the institution
2.1 Origin:
    The institutional administration .... A
    The institutional faculty (teachers) .... T
    Extra-institutional persons (outsiders) 0
  Consequence messages:
    Facilitative .... +
    Immolative .... −
    Imitative .... =
  Level of reality for change:
    Institutional commitment .... □
    Structural context .... △
    Classroom activity .... ○

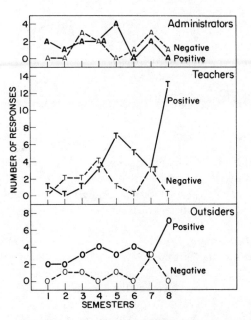

Figure 8.5. The positive and negative responses of institutional personnel to an innovation, as the responses occurred each semester over a 4-year period. Positive teacher and outsider responses show an increasing incidence of occurrence; all negative responses show a decreasing incidence of occurrence.

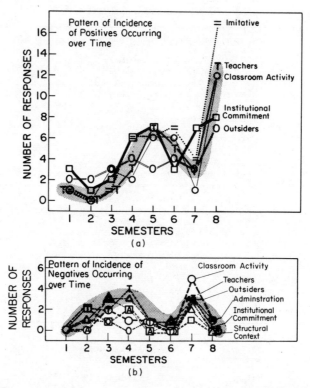

Figure 8.6. The pattern of human learning and extinction curves, characteristic of the spread of an innovation, as demonstrated by positive and negative institutional responses to an innovation over 4 years.

These three brilliantly executed studies by Chapman, Markel, and Gomon deserve careful study. If confirmed, they point to a technology of institutional change and diffusion that bears a striking similarity to the modification of work behavior of individuals, by means of discriminative learning tasks and information feedback.

Gomon's report also details the constructive value of emotional responses to an innovation. To summarize that position, an emotional attack may be viewed, first, as a response to a perceived difference and, second, as a request for information. When the crisis occurs, the innovator may flinch but must not retreat; rather, he must be ready to present the model and foils for teaching the innovative concept and have evidence of its relevance to system goals.

Stated another way, expressions of anger are common during the extinction of old behaviors. They should be viewed as indicators of change, necessary problems of the learner rather than of the behavioral engineer.

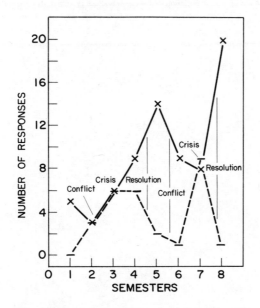

Figure 8.7. A conflict–crisis–resolution view of the repeating *X* pattern of positive and negative institutional responses to innovation. The pattern may be viewed as the meeting of conflicting positive and negative responses in a crisis, the resolution of which occasions learning of the innovation and extinction of immolative responses.

APPENDIX

TASK SYNTHESIS

Three learning paradigms will be described, one for each of the three types of learning. An analysis of substitution learning is dependent upon concepts of synthesis illustrated for Type I and Type II learning, thus will be considered later.

I. Type I: Recognition

Task Objective	Task Stimuli	Learning Operation	Criterion Test
Given X conditions, Y trainees will recognize the unit Z.	Model and target: unit. Foils: representative class members.	Given a model of Z for inspection, Y will find examples of Z embedded among foils X number of times.	Y will find Z embedded among foils an unspecified number of times.

Foils are selected so that recognition of the unit must be based upon unique characteristics. Thus, other members of the unit's class are used. They have some characteristics in common (class features), thus are maximally confusable, and

139

they differ from the unit in other characteristics (unique features). In some instances, for example, the training of inspectors for quality control tasks, foils may consist of incomplete units or units with parts disarranged.

A. *Examples*

LETTER RECOGNITION

Task Objective	Task Stimuli	Learning Operation	Criterion Test
Given printed material, first-grade children will recognize the letter *d*.	Model and target: *d*. Foils: *h, a, g, p, q, b*.	Forced choice. (Directions: Look at the one at the top. Find the same one below and circle it.)	Free choice. (Directions: Target *d* occurs one, two or three times among foils. Find it each time.)

SAMPLE FRAMES

TEST

d . . . . . . h d p q d g b a

COPY EDITING: IDENTIFYING THE COMMA-SPLICE ERROR

Task Objective	Task Stimuli	Learning Operation	Criterion Test
Given correct and incorrect sentences, college students will recognize comma-splice errors.	Sentences with connectives (which signal a semicolon), and coordinating conjunctions (which signal a comma).	Forced choice. (Directions: Look at the one at the top. Find the one like it and circle the letter.)	Free choice. (Directions: Comma-splice errors occur among correctly punctuated sentences. Find each error.)

SAMPLE FRAMES

> The hail storm was one of the most damaging in recent years; however, the cherry crop was not too severely hurt.

Which one is correct? Circle the letter.

(A) They figured it every way they knew, however, the bank statement would not balance.

(B) They figured it every way they knew; however, the bank statement would not balance.

> *Joyce was sick and tired of housekeeping; moreover, she was unhappy with her lazy husband.*

(A) *The weapons were inappropriate for modern warfare; furthermore, the soldiers' morale was low.*

(B) *The weapons were inappropriate for modern warfare, furthermore, the soldiers' morale was low.*

> *George's alarm clock failed to go off this morning, but fortunately he was not late for work.*

(A) *The young couple wanted so badly to buy the shiny red Mustang with the bucket seats, however, the price was more than they could afford.*

(B) *The young couple wanted so badly to buy the shiny red Mustang with the bucket seats, but the price was more than they could afford.*

TEST

Identify sentences with punctuation errors.

(3) *The hamburgers were delicious, but the fried chicken was not as good as usual.*

(4) *The new TV program was mercilessly panned by the critics, however, it soon became one of the most popular of the season.*

B. Decisions Required by the Paradigm

TASK OBJECTIVE

Conditions are, ideally, those obtaining in the day-to-day performance situation. For example, identifying comma-splice errors will be done during the proofreading of an essay. Thus, the conditions should include a statement such as "Given an essay in cursive writing. . . ." If that condition is not practicable, conditions must be those of the testing situation: "Given correct and incorrect sentences. . . ." Commonly, the latter decision is made.

Thus, the objective will specify the type of behavior to be required by the test and testing realities will limit the statement of objective to a realistic goal. When that goal is reached, a second objective is established: "Given an essay in cursive writing. . . ." That is, one can postpone, but not avoid, the task of bringing the new behavior under the control of field conditions.

TASK STIMULI

The unit Z is specified in the objective. The programmer determines the relevant class to which this unit belongs. Common errors ordinarily reveal the class from which foils will be selected. In the $b \cdot d$ distinction, several similar-appearing letters constitute class members. In the comma-splice program, lists of coordinating conjunctions and connectives were prepared. Correct punctuation of sentences using words from those lists provided foils.

LEARNING OPERATION

The forced-choice arrangement provides the control of the learner's attention necessary for training discriminative responses. A distinction should be made between the observing response being trained and the token response, "Circle the letter." The observing response is the object of the task. The token response requires a commitment by the learner and provides a record for the programmer.

CRITERION TEST

The form of the criterion test and the items to be used are decided before the objective is written in final form. Thus, decisions about the test influence the objective and, indirectly, the task stimuli and the learning operation.

A programmer's monolog during a task analysis may be of interest here:

Problem:	The spelling on these themes is atrocious.
Solution:	Should I program spelling?
Objective₁:	Hmmm. The objective would be to **spell certain words correctly**.
Test₁:	What will the test look like? Dictated test?
Entering behavior:	But what prior skill will that (dictated test) require? Requires good auditory discrimination. No, I can't assume that.
Test₂:	Oh, I can use the word in a dictated sentence. Requires less discrimination since they can use context clues to identify the word.
Field factors:	Is my dictation the stimulus controlling them when they write generally? No, they dictate to themselves.
Entering behavior:	What prior skill will that require? Spelling of other words. No good.
Objective₂:	Do I want them to spell correctly while writing? Yes, but as long as they copy edit before turning it in, that will do. Copy edit! Ahh. Monitoring their own reproductions. Self-shaping. Guilford's evaluation step. **Students will copy edit their papers.**

Test$_4$:   What will the test look like? A theme. Copy edit a theme for misspellings only.

In this case, the program became a copy-editing task with parts of themes as task stimuli. The form of the test clearly influences the final form of the objective.

II. Type II: Reproduction

The primary differences between the production task and Type I tasks are first, the analysis of the whole into its component parts and the arrangement of the parts (steps 2 and 4), and, second, the requirement that the parts be reproduced before the whole can be reproduced (steps 3 and 5).

Step	Task Objective	Task Stimuli	Learning Operation	Criterion Test[a]
1	Given X conditions, Y trainees will recognize the unit Z.	Model and target: unit. Foils: representative class members.	Forced choice. Given a model of Z for inspection, Y will find examples of Z embedded among foils X number of times.	Free choice. Y will find Z embedded among foils an unspecified number of times.
2	Given X conditions, Y trainees will recognize the parts of Z.	Model and target: component parts. Foils: non-parts (preferably unique parts of other class members).	Forced choice. Given a model of Z for inspection, Y will find component parts of Z embedded among foils X times.	Free choice. Y will find component parts of Z embedded among foils.
3	Given X conditions, Y trainees will reproduce the parts of Z.	Incomplete unit (one component deleted in each of several frames).	Constructed response. Given a model of Z for inspection and an incomplete unit, Y will complete the unit.	Constructed response. Y will complete an incomplete unit.

[a]A criterion test is required only at step 6. At other steps, the test may be used as a subterminal, criterion frame.

Continued

Step	Task Objective	Task Stimuli	Learning Operation	Criterion Test[a]
4	Given X conditions, Y trainees will recognize the arrangement (time or space order) of the parts of Z.	Model and target: unit (i.e., correct order of parts). Foils: alternative incorrect orders.	Forced choice. Given a model of Z, find the unit embedded among foils X times.	Free choice. Y will find Z embedded among foils.
5	Given X conditions, Y trainees will reproduce the arrangement of the parts of Z.	Component parts of Z.	Constructed response. Given a model of Z for inspection and component parts, Y will produce the order of the parts.	Constructed response. Y will order given parts.
6				On command, Y will reproduce Z.

A. *Examples*

SPELLING

Step	Directions	Learning Operations
	Use this model whenever you wish.	onomatopoeia
1	Look at the word in the box above. Find and circle it three times in the four lines.	1. omnipotent ... onomatopoeia unimportant 2. anonymous ... unimpeded ... onomatopoetic 3. onomatopoeia . omniscience .. omnivorous 4. automat ...... omniscient ... onomatopoeia
2	Find the letters of the word in order, left to right. Circle them. Now find the syllables.	zotn goami apto ipeso ewaioxra om on onom a o mat o matto poe a ia
3	Supply the missing parts.	onomatopoe_____ onomato_____ia onomat_____poeia ono_____opoeia on_____matopoeia _____omatopoeia
4	Find the word three times.	onomotopoeia onomatapoeia onomatopoeia onnomatopoeia onomatopoeia omonatopoeia onamatopoeia onomatopoeia onomatopoea
5	Unscramble the letters.	m p o t a n o i o e a o __ __ __ __ __ __ __ __ __ __ __ __

Discussion. It is not uncommon for a learner to be unable to demonstrate his new learning for a period of time after completion of the task, but to do so 1 day later without difficulty. This phenomenon bears some similarity to reminiscence, reactive inhibition, and reaction decrement. It appears to be characteristic of discrimination programming tasks.

Comment. Step 1 and step 4 tasks are similar. Foils in step 1 are members of the class, "English words that look or sound like the target." Foils in step 4 are misspellings (incorrect variants) of the target.

An appropriate requirement for **entering behavior** is familiarity with the word meaning. The form of the entering test is as follows:

Directions: Circle the word that makes sense.

> *A poetic device referring to the use of words whose sound reflects their sense is called*
>
> (alliteration/onomatopoeia).

Exiting behavior requires that the spelling be brought under the control of the usual cues operating during writing, e.g., an auto-dictated sentence in which the word is used appropriately. The form is as follows:

Directions (oral): Say a sentence using the word *onomatopoeia* in a way that reflects its meaning. Now write the sentence.

OTHER EXAMPLES

Tasks in which the time order or spatial arrangement of parts must be learned exemplify Type II tasks. Assembling complex devices; performing mechanical drawing tasks; drawing a map of any kind from memory; learning the order of colors in the spectrum, the order and target organs of spinal nerves, the chronological order of events, the order of steps in arithmetic problem solving, or proofs in geometry or deriving equations—in fact, a substantial number of school learning tasks require both recognition and reproduction of the whole, its parts, and their arrangement.

III. Type III: Substitution

A. *What Substitution Is Not*

There are two distinctions to be made between substitutions or equivalence learning tasks and those of Types I and II: First, recognition tasks are characterized by an isomorphic relationship between model and target: There is a point-for-point correspondence between the two examples of *f* in this frame:

On the other hand, the equivalence between the letter [f] and its name /eff/ is quite arbitrary, as much so as that between a man's name and his social security number. Both of these are substitution tasks.

The second distinction follows from the first: An isomorphic relationship exists in one sensory modality only. Thus Types I and II are single-modality tasks; equivalence learning may be single modality or cross modality:

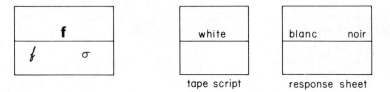

VISUAL MODALITY ONLY   **AURAL–VISUAL MODALITIES**

f	
f σ	

white	

tape script

blanc noir	

response sheet

B. *What Substitution Is*

Substitution learning is second-order learning where first-order learning consists of Type I and Type II. It assumes that responses to be substituted are already learned. With that condition, Type III is formally analogous to Type I and Type II.

To understand that statement let us return to recognition learning. Suppose the letter *d* has been contrasted with non-*d*'s, such as *b*. The learner knows something about *d* as a stimulus. We may not assume that he knows anything more about a *b* than that it is a non-*d*. The letter *b* has served as a foil; it must serve as a model also in order to be learned. Thus, all members of a class must be taught in Type I learning if they are to serve as foils in substitution tasks.

Now, let us consider a common equivalence to be learned: [f] ≡ /eff/. If we view this pair of stimuli as the **two parts of one stimulus**, [f] : /eff/, it can be treated as a Type I task. It becomes the model. The foils then consist of all confusable incorrect pairings:

MODEL

[f] : /eff/

Foils		Foils
[f] : /ee/		[l] : eff
[f] : /ss/	and	[k] : eff
[f] : /vee:		[t] : eff

The most confusable incorrect pairings are those having one term in common with the model ([f] or /eff/) and one term incorrect (such as /ee/ or [l]). The incorrect part in each foil has been chosen for its similarity to the same-modality term in the model (e.g., [l], [k], [t]).

EXAMPLE: COLOR NAMING

Objective: When presented color patches by the teacher, children (ages 4 and 5) will say the associated name.

Type I

> *Task 1:*
>
> Recognize color patches. (Discriminate color patches from one another.)
> Model and Target: Each color.
> Foils: All other colors.

Type I and Type II

> *Task 2:*
>
> Recognize and say color names. (Discriminate color *names* from one another and reproduce the names.)
>
> Target: Each color name.
> Foils: All other color names.

Type III

> *Task 3:*
>
> Say the name on presentation of the color. (Discriminate each (color patch—color name) from other combinations.)
> Target: Example: R red
> Foils:
>
> | *Class A* | | *Class B* | |
> |-----|--------|-----|-----|
> | R | orange | Y | red |
> | R | yellow | G | red |
> | R | green | B | red |

In Task 3, the color patch and its name are treated as a unit. This unit remains the target while all other incorrect combinations constitute the universe of foils.

Note that a combination may be incorrect (i.e., serve as a foil) because it has the wrong name (Class A) or because it has the wrong color patch (Class B).

A matrix illustrating targets and foils for the color naming task appears as follows:

		Red	Orange	Yellow	Green	Blue	Indigo	Violet
	R	T	F	F	F	F	F	F
	O	F	T	F	F	F	F	F
	Y	F	F	T	F	F	F	F
VISUAL	G	F	F	F	T	F	F	F
	B	F	F	F	F	T	F	F
	I	F	F	F	F	F	T	F
	V	F	F	F	F	F	F	T

AUDITORY

Legend: T = target
         F = foil

Task Stimuli (see area in matrix within broken lines):

Target: R : red

Foils: R : orange, R : yellow, R : green
          O : red, Y : red, G : red

Target: O : *orange*

Foils: O : yellow, O : green
          Y : orange, G : orange
Target: Y : yellow, and so on.

The program itself might appear in a form like the following.

Response Sheet

SCRIPT (TAPED)

Look at the box at the top.
It is red. Circle the one I say.
Number 1. RED
Number 2. YELLOW
Number 3. RED

		R	
1.	O		R
2.	R		Y
3.	R		G

The box at the top is orange.
Number 8. ORANGE
Number 9. YELLOW

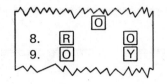

SECOND LANGUAGE TASKS

Let us assume prior auditory discrimination training in both French and English as required entering behaviors. Then,

Target : /house/·/la maison/

Foils:

Class A	Class B
/house/·/mais/	/mason/·/la maison/
/house/·/le palais/	/but/·/la maison/
/house/·/la salle/	/palace/·/la maison/

It is likely that the words from one lesson will be programmed together. Then those 10 or 15 will be treated as the universe for that lesson. Each of those words will serve as target and as a foil for every other word.

In general, however, foils are chosen from high-probability responses. The most efficient method for determining foils is to use common errors. If such evidence is unavailable, the following kinds of words are appropriate:

(*1*) words already in the learner's repertoire;
(*2*) words (in the learner's repertoire) that are similar to the target in visual or auditory characteristics;
(*3*) words (in the learner's repertoire) that are similar to the target syntactically or semantically;
(*4*) words contiguous with the target in time, i.e., appearing in the same lesson;
(*5*) words that occur as errors in the program tryout.

Substitution tasks differ from recognition and reproduction tasks in the arbitrary nature of the equivalence and in their tendency to require more than one modality. Many or most of such tasks are commonly called **associations** or **paired-associate tasks**. They may be viewed as complex discriminative learnings in which two classes of foils must be distinguished.

EXPANDED
INTERLOCKING MODEL

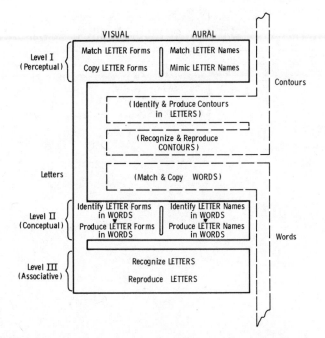

A complete unit of interlocking model. The version in Figures 3.13 and 3.14 was simplified by omitting Level II.

INSTRUCTIONAL DOMAIN FOR LANGUAGE

Content: Contours; contours in letters
Levels: Perceptual, conceptual, associative

Level I: Perceptual (in which an entity is isolated—seen, heard, felt—and copied [equiv.: recognized and reproduced])

Step A: Match

	Visual	Aural
Objective	Given an example of a contour learners will identify it among other contours.	Given the name of a contour, learners will identify it among other names of contours.

	Directions *Response Book*	*Script*	
Example	Look at the picture in the box. Find one in each line. (1. ||| (2. — (| 3. (/ ~	If the words are the same, circle *yes*. If they are different, circle *no*.	1. *Straight line . . . base line.* 2. *Curved line . . . curved line.* 3. *Short, slanted . . . short, slanted.* 4. *Vertical line . . . slanted line.*

Step B: Copy (Mime)

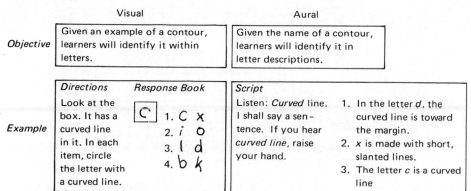

	Visual	Aural
Objective	Given an example of a contour, learners will copy it.	Given the name of a contour, learners will repeat it.

Example

Visual — *Directions* *Response Book*

Look at the box. Make one the same.

1. (curved line example)
2. (curved line example)

Aural — *Script + Visual* *Response*

This is a curved line.   (Oral)

Say: *a curved line.*

Level II: Conceptual (in which an entity is identified as a part of a larger entity and is produced in order to complete an incomplete example of that entity)

Step A: Identify

	Visual	Aural
Objective	Given an example of a contour, learners will identify it within letters.	Given the name of a contour, learners will identify it in letter descriptions.

Example

Visual — *Directions* *Response Book*

Look at the box. It has a curved line in it. In each item, circle the letter with a curved line.

1. C   x
2. *i*   o
3. l   d
4. b   k

Aural — *Script*

Listen: *Curved* line. I shall say a sentence. If you hear *curved line*, raise your hand.

1. In the letter *d*, the curved line is toward the margin.
2. *x* is made with short, slanted lines.
3. The letter *c* is a curved line

Step B: Produce, aided

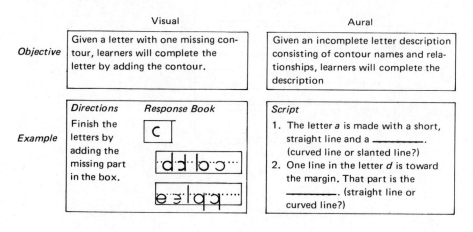

	Visual	Aural
Objective	Given a letter with one missing contour, learners will complete the letter by adding the contour.	Given an incomplete letter description consisting of contour names and relationships, learners will complete the description

Example

Visual — *Directions* *Response Book*

Finish the letters by adding the missing part in the box.

Aural — *Script*

1. The letter *a* is made with a short, straight line and a _____. (curved line or slanted line?)
2. One line in the letter *d* is toward the margin. That part is the _____. (straight line or curved line?)

Level III: Associative (in which an entity is named and reproduced)

Step A: Recognize (name, read)

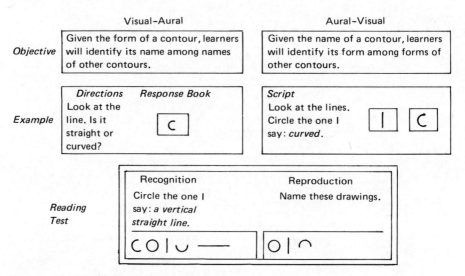

	Visual–Aural	Aural–Visual
Objective	Given the form of a contour, learners will identify its name among names of other contours.	Given the name of a contour, learners will identify its form among forms of other contours.

Example — Visual–Aural:
Directions   *Response Book*
Look at the line. Is it straight or curved? — C

Example — Aural–Visual:
Script
Look at the lines. Circle the one I say: *curved*. — | C

Reading Test

Recognition	Reproduction
Circle the one I say: *a vertical straight line.*	Name these drawings.
C O	∪ —	O	∩

Step B: Reproduce (draw, write)

Objective — Given the name of a contour, learners will identify its form among incorrect variants.

Example — Which one is a vertical line? — \ |

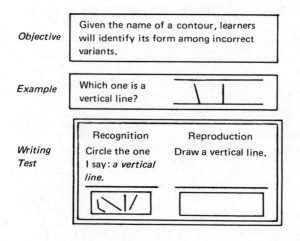

Writing Test

Recognition	Reproduction
Circle the one I say: *a vertical line.*	Draw a vertical line.
\	/	

REFERENCES

Brethower, D. M. *The classroom as a self-modifying system.* Ph.D. dissertation, University of Michigan, 1970. (Univ. Microfilm No. *31,* 2168A, 1971.)

Brethower, K. S. *Performance indicators as feedback in business settings.* Ph.D. dissertation, University of Michigan, 1973. (Univ. Microfilm No. *35,* 563B, 1975.)

Brown, J. S. Generalization and discrimination. In D. Mostofsky (Ed.), *Stimulus generalization.* Stanford: Stanford University Press, 1965.

Cabot, R. *The construction and validation of the Michigan Auditory Discrimination Test.* Unpublished Ph.D. dissertation, University of Michigan, 1968.

Chall, J. S. *Learning to read: The great debate.* New York: McGraw-Hill, 1967.

Chapman, R. E. *Evaluation as feedback in innovative school programs.* Ph.D. dissertation, University of Michigan, 1973. (Univ. Microfilm No. *34,* 1472A, 1974.)

Chomsky, C. Write first, read later. *Childhood Education,* 1971, *47,* 296–299.

Dolch, W. *A manual for remedial reading* (2nd ed.). Champaign, Ill.: Garrard, 1945.

Fernald, G. *Remedial techniques in basic school subjects.* New York: McGraw-Hill, 1943.

Foote, W. E., & Havens, L. L. Stimulus frequency: Determinant of perception or response? *Psychonomic Science,* 1965, *2,* 153–154.

Fryer, D. *Measurement of interest.* New York: Holt, 1931.

Galanter, E. *Automatic teaching: The state of the art.* New York: Wiley, 1959.

Geake, R., & Smith, D. E. P. *Visual tracking* (rev. ed.). Ferndale, Michigan: Tri Level Materials, 1975.

Gesell, A., & C. S. Amatruda. *The embryology of behavior: The beginning of the human mind.* New York: Harper, 1945.

Gibson, E. J. Perceptual learning. *Annual Review of Psychology,* 1963, *13,* 29–56.

Gibson, E. J. *Principles of perceptual learning and development.* New York: Appleton-Century-Crofts, 1969.

155

Gibson, J. J. *The senses considered as perceptual systems.* Boston: Houghton Mifflin, 1966.

Gibson, J. J., and Gibson, E. J. Perceptual learning: Differentiation or enrichment? *Psychological Review,* 1955, *62,* 32–41.

Gomon, A. *Systems communication patterns: An institution's response to an innovation.* Ph.D. dissertation, University of Michigan, 1974. (Univ. Microfilm No. *35,* 4250A, 1975.)

Goodman, K. S. Reading: A psycholinguistic guessing game. In H. Singer & R. B. Ruddell (Eds.), *Theoretical models and processes of reading.* Newark, Del.: International Reading Association, 1970.

Gould, J. D. Pattern recognition and eye-movement parameters. *Perception and Psychophysics,* 1967, *2,* 399–407.

Greene, F. P. *The effect of syntactically induced errors on retention of programmed materials.* Unpublished report, University of Michigan Center for Programmed Learning, 1967.

Guba, E. G., & Stufflebeam, D. L. *Evaluation: The process of stimulating, aiding, and abetting insightful action.* Bloomington, Ind.: Measurement and Evaluation Center, 1970.

Hebb, D. O. *The organization of behavior.* New York: Wiley, 1949.

Heiman, M. B. *Individualized instruction in the classroom.* Ph.D. dissertation, University of Michigan, 1970. (Univ. Microfilm No. *31,* 3956A, 1971.)

Hubel, D. G., & Wiesel, T. N. Receptive fields and functional architecture in the non-striate area (18 and 19) of the cat. *Journal of Neurophysiology,* 1965, *29,* 229–289.

James, W. *Principles of psychology* (Vol. 1). New York: Dover, 1950. (Originally published by Henry Holt, 1890.)

Kagan, J. On the need for relativism. *American Psychologist,* 1967, *22*(2), 131–142.

Knudsvig, G. *Cross-dialect learning.* Unpublished Ph.D. dissertation, University of Michigan, 1974.

Kopp, J. D. Generalization decrement or discrimination? The problem in the light of some recent data. In H. Lane (Ed.), *Studies in language and language behavior* (Progress Report No. 1). University of Michigan, Center for Research on Language and Language Behavior, 1965.

Labov, W. Some sources of reading problems for Negro speakers of nonstandard English. In J. Baratz & R. Shuy (Eds.), *Teaching black children to read.* Washington, D.C.: Center for Applied Linguistics, 1969.

Lashley, K. S., & Wade, M. The Pavlovian theory of generalization. *Psychological Review,* 1946, *53,* 72–87.

Latour, P. L. Visual threshold during eye movement. *Vision Research,* 1962, *2,* 261.

Llewellyn Thomas, E. Movements of the eye. *Scientific American,* 1968, *219,* 88–95.

Mackworth, N. H., & E. L. Thomas. *Journal of the Optical Society of America. 52* (1962) 713–716.

Markel, G. *The evaluation consultant and innovative elementary projects in an educational system.* Ph.D. dissertation, University of Michigan, 1974. (Univ. Microfilm No. *35,* 2774A, 1975.)

Markle, S. M. *Words: A programmed course in vocabulary development.* Chicago: Science Research Associates, 1968.

Markle, S. M. *Good frames and Bad: A grammar of frame writing* (2nd ed.), New York: Wiley, 1969.

McConnell, J. Criminals can be brainwashed, now! *Psychology Today,* April 1970, pp. 14–16.

INDEX

A

Adaptive System
  awareness of consequences, 121
  defined, 123 ff
  feedback, 44
  ingredients of, 20
  language learning laboratory, 132
  self-shaping, 120
Amatruda, C. S., 55
Attending
  as motivation, 115 ff
  auditory training and, 90
  control of, by foils, 29, 63, 64, 73, 74
  distractions, 116
  focusing, as zoom lens, 81
  performance deficiencies and, 19 ff
  to pictures, 8
  to spaces between words, 63
Auditory discrimination, *see* Discrimination

B

Basic skills, *see* Subroutines
Behavioral engineering
  as behavior modification, 118 ff
  assumptions, 5
  defined, 1, 3
  iterative development in, 52 ff, 100
  measurement in, 99 ff
  paradigm, 15
  programming strategy, 67, 86
  school innovations, 125 ff
  stimulus control, 27, 29, 63, 73, *see also*
    Attending
  task requirements for, 63
Brethower, D.M., 20, 22, 121, 122,
    123 ff
Brethower, K.S., 121, 122
Brown, J.S., 32
Burr, K., 87

C

Cabot, R., 16, 20, 42, 90, 121
Carrigan, P., 127
Chall, J.S., 110
Chapman, R.E., 118, 121, 122, 125, 126
Chomsky, C., 56
Cross-modality, *see* Information processing

D

Decoding
  distortions, 17
  process, 2, 13
  stages, example of, 101
Discrimination
  auditory, 15, 16, 17, 23, 45, 88, 89
  errors, as failure of, 33
  generalization, as failure of, 32
  letters, 25 ff, *see also* Letters
  model of learning, 133
  of letter features *see* Discrimination
      learning, discriminanda
  of space, 64
  training in, 74, 86 ff
  visual, 17, 18
Discrimination learning
  apparent, within system, 129 ff
  arrangement of parts, 30 ff, 50, 52, 53, 64
  conditions for, 37 ff., 63
  discriminanda, 30, 32, 38, 51, 63, 73, 74
  examples, 1
  facts, 39
  forced choice–free choice, 9 ff
  of pictures, 7–10
  of target, 61
  stages of, 100 ff
  types of, 27, 31 ff
Distinctive characteristics (features), *see*
      Discrimination learning, discriminanda
Dolch, E., 13
Domains
  of language, 4
  of skills, 99 ff
Durrell, D., 78

E

Effectors, 46
Equivalence, *see* Learning target, substitu-
      tion

Eye movements
  during reading, 70 ff
  microfixations, 71
  micromovements, 71
  visual excursions, 19, 25, 60, 67

F

Feedback, *see* Information processing
Fernald, G., 60, 77
Fryer, D., 16

G

Galanter, E., 5
Geake, R., 19, 86
Gesell, A., 55
Gibson, E.J., 32
Gibson, J.J., 29, 32, 64, 78
Gomon, A., 121, 125, 129 ff.
Goodman, K.S., 19, 73
Gould, J.D., 74
Greene, F.P., 51
Guba, E.G., 125

H

Hallucinatory image, 46, 74, 80, 81, 88
Havens, L.L., 74
Hebb, D., 47, 78, 79
Heiman, M.B., 43, 121
House, B.J., 43
Hubel, D.G., 73

I

Identification tasks, 46 ff, 81
Independent learning
  motivation, and, 115 ff
  repetition, and, 64
  constituents, 4
Information processing
  central processing, 67 ff
  circuitry for, 82 ff
  cross-modality, 44 ff, 64 ff
  defined, 68 ff
  failure of, in low intelligence, 41 ff
  feedback, 20 ff, 26, 44 ff, 50, 51, 52, 118,
      121 ff, 127
  input–output, 11
  mechanisms of, 79 ff

of language, 4
of reading and writing, 77 ff
of stimuli, 60 ff
single-modality, 44 ff, 64 ff
storage, 79
system, 44 ff, 121 ff
uncertainty, and, 62, 63, 69, 74, 79 ff,
  115 ff
Interlocking model, 55 ff
  expanded, 151 ff
  skill domain, and, 102 ff

J

James, W., 79

K

Kagan, J., 32
Knudsvig, G., 18, 36, 37
Kopp, J.D., 32

L

Language
  concept, teaching of, 53, 54
  dialect, 36, 38
  domain, 53, 57, 102 ff
  learning, 26, 27
  structures, in interlocking model, 55
Language Arts Competency Profile,
  105–109
Lashley, K.S., 32
Latour, P.L., 70
Learning
  by a school system, 133
  defined, 61
  emotionality, and, 136
  repetition in, 64
  uncertainty, and, 62
Learning target
  defined, 27 ff, 61, 70
  dialect, 18, 36, 38
  model, 51
  recognition of, 27, 31 ff, 46 ff, 65 ff
  reproduction of, 27, 31 ff, 46 ff, 65 ff, 88
  self-shaping, and, 4
  substitution of, 27, 31 ff, 65 ff
Learning to read
  auditory discrimination in, 16 ff
  decoding, 13 ff, 53, 94

defined, 21
phonograms, 13
pictures, 7–10
process, 7 ff, 57, 67 ff, 74
sequence, 53 ff, 57
task requirements, 63 ff
verbal fluency, 18, 91
versus reading, 2
Learning to write
  algorithm, 84
  as copy-editing, 52, 140–142
  name, 88
  process, 7 ff, 19
  space discrimination, and, 64
  spelling, 64, 144
Letters
  as target, 61
  contours, 49, 50, 53
  drawing, 87 ff
  features, 63
  matching, 52
  names, 49, 50, 54, 56, 84–85, 91
Listening, defined, 28
Llewellyn, Thomas, E., 71, 74

M

Mackworth, N., 51
Markel, G., 118, 121, 125, 127 ff
Markle, S.M., 51
McConnell, J., 119
Memory
  auditory, 73
  short-term, 46
Michigan Language Program, 54, 65, 67, 87,
  90, 91, 93, 95, 96
Motivation
  as attention, 113 ff
  as awareness of consequences, 121
  feedback, and, 20

O

Objectives, 47 ff
Olds, R.E., 43, 121, 122

P

Paired-associate learning, *see* Learning
  target, substitution

Paradigm
  color naming, 147
  copy editing, 52, 140
  cross-modality, 50, 64 ff
  directions, 96
  generalized, 139, 152 ff
  in interlocking model, 56
  learning to read, 8 ff
  letter drawing, 89
  letter naming, 85–86
  matching to sample, 38, 39, 51, 52
  phonics, 94
  second language, 149
  sentence meanings, 95
  single-modality, 48, 49
  spelling, 144
  subroutines, 85 ff
  substitution, 36 ff, 65 ff
Phonics, *see* Learning to read, decoding
Pike, K.L., 78, 102
Powers, W. T., 118
Premack, D., 45
Processes
  teaching tasks, and, 51 ff
  versus answers, 50, 51
Producing system, *see* Information processing
Production
  auditory, 18
  visual, 19

Q

Questions, 70

R

Reading
  defined, 24, 69
  problems, *see* Reading problems
Reading problems
  dependency, 115 ff
  directionality, 92
  directions, 96
  emotionality, and, 62
  intelligence, and, 41 ff
  letter naming, 91
  letter recognition, 85–86
  oral, and visual excursions, 19, 25 ff, 60, 71, ff

  passive–aggressive, 20
  paying attention, 90
  rule-testing, 117
  sentence meaning, 95
  task deficiencies, and, 48 ff
  word calling, 19
  word fluency, 91
  work output, 120
Receiving system, *see* Information processing
Rule-testing, 117, 119, 122

S

Samuels, S.J., 15
Scriven, M., 125
Self-modifying system, *see* Adaptive system
Self-shaping system, *see* Adaptive system
Semmelroth, C., 19, 68 ff, 71, 72, 74, 93
Sequencing, *see* Discrimination learning, arrangement of parts
Single-modality, *see* Information processing
Skinner, B.F., 3, 26, 64, 78, 119, 120
Smith, D.E.P., 18, 19, 20, 38, 53, 54, 65, 67, 71, 72, 84, 86, 89, 90, 118, 119, 121
Smith, **J.M.**, 53, 54, 65, 67, 84, 90, 91, 118, 119
Smith, P.H., 19
Sommer, B., 19, 29, 88
Sounding, *see* Decoding
Speaking
  defined, 24
  as output, 45 ff
Specious present, 78
Spelling, *see also* Writing
  letter names, and, 12, 64
  paradigm, 144
Stress, 73, 116
Stuart, R.B., 122
Stufflebeam, D.L., 125
Subroutines (basic skills)
  deficiencies, 15
  tasks, and, 48
  teaching, 85 ff

T

Tagmemics, 102
Task analysis, 34

Tasks
    characteristics, 48 ff, 117 ff
    iterative development of, 52, 53
    matching to sample, 51, 62, 63
Taylor, S.E., 70
Tests
    criterion-referenced, 100 ff
    norm-referenced, 99
Trotter, S., 119
Tutorphonics, 95

V

Visual Tracking, 52, 85, 86, 87
Volkman, F.C., 70

W

Wade, M., 32
Walter, T.L., 121, 122
Warren, J., 119
Whole–part, *see* Learning to read
Wiesel, T.N., 73
Wiig, E.H., 19
Word analysis, *see* Decoding
Writing, *see also* Letters
    as information, 45 ff
    defined, 24

Z

Zeaman, D., 43

Date